WARRING
with
THE WORD

Stay on fire for Jesus.

Shawn Patrick Williams

SHAWN PATRICK WILLIAMS

DEDICATION

This book is dedicated to my wife, Christy Williams. Throughout all the battles, lessons, and victories, you have been by my side. You have grabbed hold of our vision and run with it with all your might. You have been the world's best partner, mother, and wife, but most of all, you have been the best friend that anyone could ever hope for. I love you so much!

Shawn Patrick Williams

Shawn Patrick Williams

TABLE OF CONTENTS

A WORD FROM THE AUTHOR

The purpose of this book is to assist the believer in a victorious Christian lifestyle. The only way a Christian can live a victorious Christian lifestyle is to know Christ. Too many people see Christianity as method or a system to follow in order to solve their problems and save themselves from eternal judgment. True Christianity isn't based on religious traditions, or "good works," but on having a personal relationship with Jesus Christ through His Holy Spirit. No other foundation will stand when the waves of life's trials and temptations come smashing against your house.

Standing against life's trials and temptations for yourself, or for others is what most people refer to when they talk about "spiritual warfare." Whether these trials or temptations are self-induced or brought about by a spiritual force, as believers we must stand! The only way to successfully stand is on the Word of God! Any teaching on spiritual warfare that does not teach you how to hurl the sword of the Spirit, will only leave you tired, disappointed, and defeated. Imagine being in a sword fight with only protective armor and no offensive weapon to bring about a piercing blow to your enemy. You will constantly be taking blows and eventually be worn down by your enemy and be defeated.

True, lasting, successful spiritual warfare is based on faith in Jesus Christ and faith in the ability of His Word. This is the place of rest spoken of in Hebrews 4. As you read this book, I pray you find that place of rest in a victorious Christian lifestyle.

Pastor Shawn Patrick Williams

Warring With The Word

"I have written unto you, young men, because ye are strong, and the word of God abideth in you, and ye have overcome the wicked one." I John 2:14

CHAPTER ONE

ENLISTED FOR SERVICE

Have you ever had a moment in your life when you stopped, looked around, and thought, "how did I get here"? On August 16, 1998, I looked around and found myself surrounded by leaders from the church of Satan and from the Santeria occult. I was about to be inducted into the army of Satan. For the first time in my life I could see what I was becoming and it scared me to death! Or should I say it scared me to life!

"And they (the Saints) overcame him (Satan) by the blood of the Lamb, and by the word of their (the Saints) testimony; and they loved not their lives unto the death" Revelation 12:11.

There is a spiritual release when a believer shares his testimony with others. Part of your spiritual warfare armor is giving your testimony. Ephesians 6:15 says to "have your feet shod with the preparation of the gospel of peace." Be prepared to share with others how Jesus has changed your life. It will energize your relationship with Jesus Christ, because the Holy Spirit will empower you to testify.

Right now, I want to share my testimony with you and tell you how I received deliverance from drug addiction, sexual bondage, occultism, and many other issues by fighting with the written Word of God. By using the Holy Scriptures, I received complete freedom from satanic bondage and occultic ties.

The first thing you must understand is that I grew up in a Christian home and spent most of my school years in a Christian school. I heard someone preaching the Bible every day of my life. The memorization of scripture was part of my academic curriculum. The problem wasn't a lack of hearing the Word; the problem was actually taking that knowledge and activating it into my life mixed with faith.

You see, I knew about Jesus, but I didn't have a personal relationship with Him. At the age of 7, I came down to the altar, said a prayer of salvation, and joined the church. There was nothing wrong with the prayer of salvation I prayed. The problem was my understanding of what salvation was. I thought if I said this magic prayer, it was my ticket into Heaven. I thought I could come to church, clock in and clock out, leave and continue to live in sin, with no change. Christianity is not like that; it's a lifestyle!

At the age of 13, I felt the call into ministry on my life, but there was a problem. My foundation was based on religion and not a relationship with Jesus. When life's trials and temptations came, my foundation crumbled! I started making poor choices about where I would go and what I would do. By the age of 14, I was tripping (getting high on LSD). By the age of 17, when my parents divorced, I was a drug addict, and I was living on the streets.

On my 18th birthday on a beach in Jacksonville, Florida, discouraged by life, and disappointed by what I thought was God, I cursed God and made a vow to Satan. Little did I realize the magnitude of the door I opened that moment. Soon after that night I became very ambitious concerning selling drugs. I moved in with a group that was involved into Wiccanism, which is like Paganism. I was selling drugs to all different types of people and in all different types of places. Some of the types of people were heavily involved in witchcraft, such as Satanism and Santeria. Some of them were involved in the Mexican and Dixie Mafia. Others were involved in Hell's Angels, and I also had contact with lots of well-known band members such as 311 and Widespread Panic.

During these years, I grew really close to a preacher in the church of Satan. The Reverend and a high priest in Santeria mentored me. Throughout this time, I saw crazy things. One day in particular, I saw a guy in the Dixie Mafia who was involved in witchcraft release a lightning like power source from his fingertips (similar to the movie *X-Men 1.5*). My friends involved in Santeria and Satanism would actually "bless" night clubs and businesses in the Atlanta area with spells and incantations. I actually saw two of my roommates who were involved in a satanic band become possessed by demons, speak to each other in an unknown tongue, and then question me about my views on sin. While living with Satanists in a warehouse, the demonic oppression was so strong that while under the influence of cocaine I actually drank my own blood, and I did so without knowing why I was doing it.

After five years of this lifestyle, my brother asked me to help him establish a bar and grill in South Carolina. I wasn't exactly trilled about leaving the fast-paced lifestyle of Atlanta, but I knew I needed change. Before I left, the Santeria priest released many incantations through spells, stones, herbs, and tarot cards over me, my brother, and the business we were about to establish. For the next two years of my life, the bar and grill prospered, and so did the drug business. In the middle of all this success that I had longed for as a teenager came a very heavy price to pay. I had become a very paranoid, greedy, and miserable drug addict. Snorting, shooting cocaine, and eating as many hits of ecstasy or acid as I could without overdosing, I started to flirt with suicide.

The more destructive my behavior became, the greater my desire became to be a part of this occultic network. I realized that my ties to these people stemmed from that night on the beach in Jacksonville, Florida. During this time a demon spirit started revealing himself to me. He began tempting me with ideas about ruling the underworld and the business world through its demonic power.

On my 25th birthday, seven years to the day of that night on the beach, I drove to Atlanta to surprise my friends and celebrate my birthday. I was the one in for the biggest surprise on this night. When I got to the club, one of the most popular rave bars in Atlanta at that time, all my friends in this network were waiting for me. I told no one that I was traveling out of the state that night. Friends from all over the country just happened to be there this night.

Toward the end of the night my mentor, the Satanic High Priest, walked me into the DJ booth to show me something. He pointed over a sea of people dancing and asked me to look at their new "art work." As I looked over the crowd, I saw a painting of a dark angel with its wings spread, and in the corner I saw a dark outline of Jesus. Nobody else could see the paintings unless they were in the DJ booth. The dark Reverend turned around, looked me in the eyes, and with his hands wide open made an offer of partnership in his business, and to be a brother in his network.

At the very moment that he turned around with his arms wide open and looked me in the eyes a voice spoke to me and said, "Heaven is real, Hell is real, and you have to make a choice." I became completely conscious of my spiritual state. The drugs and alcohol seemed to fade away, and conviction from the Holy Spirit was the only thing on my mind. I spent the rest of the night listening to my mentor tell me his master plan of how we were going to become millionaires within a year, but all I could think about was getting back to South Carolina and finding that old dusty Bible that I had packed away years ago.

On August 16, 1998, I made a choice to serve God no matter what. I went to the Lord in prayer and told Him I would serve Him however He wanted me to; but, I had problems, and I wanted to be completely free from all satanic bondage. I immediately started reading the Bible day and night. Every time the desire to do drugs, commit a sexual sin, or any temptation that came around, I would pull out that old Bible, and start reading the Word out loud. No matter what temptation or trial came my way, the Word of God brought me victory. Every hex, every vex, and every spell that was on my life was broken by faith in the power of God's Word.

I was so determined to be free that I would take the Bible with me into my bar and grill. I would read it between serving beers to customers. My friends would come up and cut lines of cocaine on the bar, tempting me, but the power of God's Holy Word kept me steadfast. I received my complete deliverance from drugs, alcohol, and all satanic bondage through the Word with absolutely no D.T.s or side effects. And I have kept my deliverance through the Word.

After leaving Atlanta that night, I never tried to call or contact any of those friends again. I began to fast and to pray for their salvation. Over the next six months, I experienced extreme demonic oppression. Demons started to manifest themselves in my home, telling me they were going to kill me. They were trying to scare me. People would astral project into my home, trying to influence my mind through witchcraft and spy on what I was doing. Astral projecting is when people, through witchcraft, travel out of their body in a spirit form. Through prayer, fasting, and the Word of God, I received complete victory from all spiritual warfare.

One year later I found out that the night club they owned had completely shut down. Every person involved in that network had disappeared from the area. The high priest of the Santeria cult threw himself in front of an Atlanta MARTA transit bus; however, he did not die. When I prayed for these people, I wanted to see them changed by God; I did not want to see them dead. One new Christian, filled with God's Spirit and quoting God's Word, can shut down a whole occultic network. Praise the Lord, all things are possible with God!

You are the righteousness of God in Christ Jesus and a child of the Most High God. The only way Satan can defeat you is through your sin or your lack of knowledge. Learn to stand on God's Word, and see His promises and your destiny come to pass in your life today!

CHAPTER TWO

BATTLEFIELD LESSONS

"ISOLATION AND IGNORANCE"

Picture this! It's 1968. You are 18 years old and you've just gotten out of boot camp after being drafted into the army. You've been dropped behind enemy lines in Vietnam. Your squad has just been ambushed and most of them killed by the Viet Cong. You have lost all contact with anyone. You're in the middle of the jungle, by yourself, surrounded by Viet Cong. And you are scared and have no clue what to do.

You are isolated and ignorant and this is exactly where Satan wants you.

This is exactly how I felt the first few months after I left my life in the underworld. I was alone, still working with my brother, managing our bar and grill. I wasn't in church and I didn't know anything about Jesus or His Word. I knew He was real and that He died on the cross for my sins that I might live forever, but that was about it.

I was scared my friends from the occult might try to come after me in some way. I didn't know if I could survive in an environment full of drugs, alcohol, and all the other things that come with the lifestyle. I didn't feel that any person could possibly know the things that I was going through at the time. If I tried to tell my family, they would think I was crazy.

Satan thrives on the children of God when they get into similar situations. I Peter 5:8 says, "Be sober, be vigilant, because your adversary the devil, as a roaring lion, walketh about, seeking whom he may devour." Have you ever watched *Wild Kingdom* and seen how lions single out their prey. They watch the flock very carefully, singling out the sheep that start to lag behind the group. Once the sheep fall far enough behind, the lion takes full advantage of their isolation and pounces on his prey.

Satan does the same thing when he plots against the children of God. Just like the lion, he will wait until you become isolated and disconnected from the flock and then attack. Do you know the number one reason most new believers might turn back into a life of sin? Often they are isolated from other believers.

Not only does Satan want to keep you isolated, he wants to keep you ignorant. A person will never operate beyond his/her knowledge base. Hosea 4:6 says, "My people are destroyed for lack of knowledge." What you don't know *can* hurt you.

The first few months after my salvation experience, I was not in church and I didn't know a great deal about the Word. I was very vulnerable when it came to spiritual warfare. I did not understand who I was in Jesus Christ. And every demon on assignment took full advantage of my lack of knowledge. In the spirit, I stuck out like a sore thumb.

During this time I had been reading my Bible, but I was having a hard time understanding and remembering the scriptures. I knew that I had stayed completely free from drug addiction and other sins I was previously in bondage to before I got saved, and I knew my freedom was because of the Word of God.

Before I was saved, these sins had overpowered me and entangled my life. I was not aware of the bondage until after I was saved. After I was saved, I stopped acting on all the previous sins and was ten times more sensitive to the temptations of the sins because of the gift of discernment. My mind was being purified by the water of the washing of the Word, and sin stuck out like blood in snow. I thought I was going crazy because of the mental attacks on my mind. Demonic manifestations became almost a common occurrence in my apartment. Night-time was the worst. I would be tormented by thoughts of fear and, finally, after I would fall asleep, I would have nightmares all night only to wake up to my bed levitating an inch or two off the ground.

"OVERCOMING FEAR!"

Sometimes there would be physical manifestations of demons, but one thing was for sure: I was a new person and free from the bondage of sin. Every time I called the name of Jesus, all the demonic attacks ceased for a while, and the demons would leave reluctantly.

I knew my situation was serious and that I needed breakthrough in my life. Being alone and ignorant of the spirit world, I needed help! After three months of this spiritual stalemate, one morning two demonic beings manifested at the foot of my bed. I looked up to see two semi-transparent silhouettes so tall that their heads nearly touched the ceiling. They looked like something from the Arnold Schwarzenegger movie, *The Predator*. I could see them vaguely, but still see through them. My bedroom was filled with an atmosphere of terror. As I looked in horror, one of them said, "We are going to kill you."

At this point I was sick and tired of living in fear and I began to notice that, although I was more aware of these attacks, they couldn't control or hurt me. They had been able to use fear only to scare me. I had also noticed that before I was saved, they weren't as visible, and they had more control over my life. After I received Christ as my Savior, they kept their distance from me and used tactics of fear and intimidation. I knew there was a reason they wouldn't come near me.

Satan's kingdom is the opposite of God's kingdom. Satan has no creative power. He can only pervert what God has created. Satan himself was created by God. God's kingdom operates on faith, while Satan's operates on fear. Fear is a dominant factor in Satan's kingdom. Satan will try to use fear in spiritual warfare, and usually it is his first tactic.

Romans 8:15 says, "For ye have not received the spirit of bondage again to fear; but ye have received the Spirit of adoption, whereby we cry, Abba, Father." As children of God we can be completely free from fear because we are children of the Most High God. The Psalms tell us we can serve God without fear. Once you begin to understand your authority as a believer, you will become completely free from fear. When you do, watch out! You will start to see major victory in your life as a believer.

At the point that these two beings threatened to kill me, a holy boldness rose up from within me. I rose from my bed, and with authority yelled at the top of my lungs, "If you kill me, I'm going to Heaven and you are not. So leave in the name of Jesus!" Immediately both creatures disappeared. Then the room filled with the peace of God. From that point on, the demonic manifestations began to stop and I began to see how powerful God really was in my life.

I began to praise God daily, talk to Him like two friends would talk, and read the Word from the time I would get home until I would fall asleep. Many nights I would fall asleep reading the Bible and wake up the next morning on top of the Word. One night as I was talking to God in my bedroom, I felt something on the top of my head. It felt like something was being torn from the center of my brain. It hurt, but for some reason I knew that it was from God. I couldn't explain it, but I had the peace of God. For the next five to ten minutes this went on. All of a sudden, in the very same place that I felt the tearing, an electric, euphoric feeling filled every single molecule of me. I could only cry and praise God! It felt like electric glory! The Bible describes this feeling as "rivers of living water."

As the weeks went by, the more I prayed, fasted, and read the Word, the deeper this glory went into my body. Eventually the glory consumed my whole body. As I began to ask God what was happening to me, He told me that He had taken me personally through what was known as "deliverance." This is commonly referred to as an exorcism.

During this time I was still managing the bar and grill. So, the transition from work to home was always tough spiritual warfare. I would read the Bible in the bar while serving alcohol to customers. I never preached to them or anything like that, but I knew if I was going to truly stay free from sin in this environment, I would have to go to the extreme. Every time a demonic manifestation would start, I would quote one of the two scriptures I had memorized and they would stop.

By my sixth month of being saved, God supernaturally led me to a church that preached the uncompromised Word of God. People could worship God without any restraint. It was very liberating and encouraging to know I wasn't the only Christian who had a relationship with God like this. As these months went by, I started to see greater victory in spiritual warfare then ever before. God would pour out His Spirit anywhere and answer all types of prayers from the biggest to the smallest.

On one occasion, I could see demonic manifestations, but no angelic manifestations. The Lord told me that His holy angels where humble and did not want to take any glory away from Him, but the demons were very prideful and wanted you to focus on them so they could receive perverted honor and glory. He said my focus should not be on demons, but Him and His Word. He also said that if they tried to manifest I should take authority over them in the name of Jesus and they would leave.

My relationship with Christ started to become like that shared by best friends. I stopped managing the bar and grill and started fellowshipping with other believers. Spiritually, I had ultimate peace. There were still demonic attacks and manifestations, but they were not as frequent and did not last as long.

"HOUSE CLEANING"

The Holy Spirit prompted me to clean my house from all occultic objects. This was a process. Through teaching from my church and my own personal experiences, I learned that the reason these demonic manifestations where happening was because there were "open doors" in my apartment. I prayed over my house many times and did some spiritual house cleaning.

Ephesians 4:27 says, "Neither give place[1] to the devil." The scripture actually should have been translated, "Neither give the devil a place to stand." You see, Satan has to have a legal right to operate. Whether it is unrepented sin in your life or an occultic object in your presence, he has to have a right to operate.

One night, during a full moon, I was moving furniture around in my apartment in preparation for a move into a new house. As I was moving a bedroom dresser, I found a black leather lip stick case with a crystal in it. Two years before, I had had a relationship with a girl whom I had gotten pregnant. She had an abortion. During the abortion her best friend, who was a Wiccan witch, cast a spell in order to catch the spirit of the unborn baby and put in the crystal.

After the abortion, she gave the crystal to me in a black leather lip stick case and told me what she had done. So, two years later, I find this crystal under the bedroom dresser. I am a new creature in Christ now. I did not understand that once a baby dies, its spirit goes back to God. I picked up the black leather case and opened it. I took out the crystal and held it firmly in my right hand as I remembered my unborn child and the circumstances. As I began to meditate on the whole situation, an evil presence started to manifest in the hand in which I was holding the crystal. I could feel it start to go up my arm and spread to the rest of my body. I immediately dropped the crystal on the floor and rebuked the spirit in the name of Jesus over and over again.

I then called a friend from the church I was attending and told him what had just happened to me. He told me to hold on and he would call someone from the church leadership to counsel me. When the leadership called, God had already told this person the name of this demonic spirit. Through a word of knowledge, the name that the Lord identified was "Molech," the god of child sacrifice in the Old

Testament.[2] I repented of my part in the situation, took authority over Molech, cast it out of my apartment, and got rid of the black case and the crystal. Once I did these things, the peace and presence of God was quickly ushered back into my apartment.

Spiritual house cleaning is an ongoing process. There are many different instances where other people "open doors" through the television or the internet. As in times past, I would have to pray and ask God why these demonic forces where able to be in my house. God would then show me their "legal right" of entrance.

Deuteronomy 7:25-26 says, "The graven images of their gods shall ye burn with fire: thou shalt not desire the silver or gold that is on them, nor take it unto thee, lest thou be snared therein: for it is an abomination to the Lord thy God, neither shalt thou bring an abomination into thine house, lest thou be a cursed thing like it: but thou shalt utterly detest it, and thou shalt utterly abhor it; for it is a cursed thing."

God clearly warns us in His Word to keep our houses clean from all occultic objects. Talismans, music, movies, or anything else that could be tied to the occult are harmful. If you fail to believe and obey, a curse will come upon your home, your family, and your life.

During this first year of my Christian life there were many battlefield lessons that I experienced that you can avoid. Avoiding isolation from Christians, reading and quoting God's Word, overcoming fear, and keeping your home as well as body (God's temple) clean are excellent starts to living a lasting victorious Christian lifestyle that God intended for you to live.

God has given you His Word and empowered you with the precious Holy Spirit. He will keep you and guide you into all truth. "Trust in the Lord with all thine heart; and lean not unto thine own understanding. In all thy ways acknowledge him, and he shall direct thy paths" Proverbs 3:5-6.

Notes

[1]Strong, James (1990). *The New Strong's Exhaustive Concordance of the Bible*. Nashville, TN: Thomas Nelson, Inc. tŏpŏs (#5117)Greek.

[2]Ryrie, Charles Caldwell (1976, 1978). *The Ryrie Study Bible*. King James Version of the Bible. Chicago, Illinois: Moody Press Chicago. Leviticus Chapter 20.

Shawn Patrick Williams

CHAPTER THREE

IT IS WRITTEN

From the very beginning of time, Satan's attacks on God's people haven't necessarily been focused on God's people as much as it has been focused on what God's Word says about God's people. One thing you must understand is that Satan has been around for a long time. He remembers when God spoke the worlds into existence through His Word. Hebrews 11:3 explains that "through faith we understand that the worlds were framed by the word of God, so that things which are seen were not made of things which do appear." The whole universe operates on God's Word and the authority that is behind that Word. As a matter of fact, "heaven and earth will pass away, but God's word will never pass away" Matthew 5:18.

Satan knows this. He is aware of the power and authority of God's Word. When you study God's Word, there is something you need to remember: It is called the principle of first things. This principle works when something happens first in the Word and then sets tones and patterns through out the rest of the Bible revealing Kingdom principles to the believer.

Let's use this principle in relation to how Satan tries to attack the power and authority of God's Word. In Genesis 3:1-6 it says, "Now the serpent was more subtle than any beast of the field which the Lord God had made. And he (the serpent) said unto the woman, Yea, hath God said, Ye shall not eat of every tree of the garden? And the woman said unto the serpent, We may eat of the fruit of the trees of the garden: But of the fruit of the tree which is in the midst of the garden, God hath said, Ye shall not eat of it, neither shall you touch it, lest ye die. And the serpent said unto the woman, YE SHALL NOT SURELY DIE: For God doth know that in the day ye eat thereof, then your eyes shall be opened, and ye shall be as gods, knowing good and evil. And when the woman saw that the tree was good for food, and that it was pleasant to the eyes, and a tree to be desired to make one wise, she took of the fruit thereof, and did eat, and gave also unto her husband with her; and he did eat."

As soon as Satan showed up in the Book of beginnings, the very first thing he said was, "Yea, hath God said?" The very first action he took was to discredit the Word of God. If Satan can get you to disregard God's Word, he doesn't have to do anything else. You do the rest.

Satan will always try to get your focus off God's Word and on his words, and eventually onto his plan. Genesis 3:6 says, "And when the woman <u>saw</u> that the tree was for food, and that it was pleasant to the eyes, and a tree to be desired to make one wise, she took of the fruit."

The Hebrew word for "saw" in this verse is râ'âh,[1] and it literally means to stare or look on. If Satan can get you to stare, or look on what he says about your circumstance rather than what God has said about your circumstance, then he knows that you are already defeated. Satan will always try to get you to operate on your own power and authority instead of God's authority and power, which is manifested through His Word. This has been the plan since the beginning, and I mean way back in the beginning.

"BEYOND THE BEGINNING"

The entire Kingdom of Heaven operates on God's Word. The angels operate on the authority of God's Word, not beyond it. Satan used the same method he used on Eve as he did in Heaven when he deceived 1/3 of the angels into disobedience. I can hear him now. "You don't have to obey God's Word. He just doesn't want you to be like Him." One third of the angels looked on the word of Satan rather than on obeying

God's Word, and it cost them their residence in Heaven.

Even Michael, the warring archangel, was tempted to operate beyond God's Word. Jude 9 says, "Yet Michael the archangel, when contending with the devil he disputed about the body of Moses, durst not bring against him a railing accusation, but said, The Lord rebuke thee." The book of Jude gives us a close look at a confrontation between Michael and the devil. Verse 9 says that Michael contended with the devil. This word "contend" literally means to oppose, to hesitate, to stagger, or to waiver.[2] This tells us Michael was arguing with Satan about the bones of Moses and had some difficulty. Michael had a struggle. Why? Because Satan was trying to get Michael to fight him in his own power rather than the authority of God's Word. Angels receive a word from God and carry out that word. They don't go beyond the authority of the Word God gave them for their assignment. Satan tried to move Michael off the Word given to him for his assignment. Michael would not bring an accusation against Satan, but said, "The Lord rebuke thee." When Michael stood back on the Word and the authority of God, he received the victory. Praise God!

Even the angels have been through the temptation of operating outside the Word of God. Those that chose not to obey God's Word and authority faced the same consequences as Adam and Eve did in the

Garden of Eden. The fallen angels and Adam and Eve were separated from the presence of God. It was not God's will for the angels, nor man to be separated from His presence.

One thing you must understand is that God's presence is His Spirit and the Spirit of God is subject to the Word of God. Even the Holy Spirit works in harmony with the Word of God. In fact, the Holy Spirit will respond only to God's Word and never go beyond the Word.

Genesis 1:2 says, "And the earth was without form, and void; and darkness was upon the face of the deep. And the Spirit of God moved upon the face of the waters." We don't know how many years take place between Genesis 1:1 and 1:2. It could have been one hundred thousand or ten thousand years, but the fact remains there were many years in between the two verses. Most scholars believe this was the time period in which the dinosaurs lived on earth. Genesis 1:3 reads, "And God said, Let there be light; and there was light." We don't know how many years are in between 1:2 and 1:3, but whether it was one hour or one hundred thousand years, the Spirit of God hovered over the earth and did nothing. He just hovered and waited! The Holy Spirit of God hovered and waited for the Word of God.

And God said, "Let there be light," and the Holy Spirit displayed the first light show on earth. Streaks of light sent a blinding glare off the water! The Holy Spirit didn't even move until He got a Word from the Lord and He still didn't move without the Word.

Now the same Holy Spirit lives inside man's heart and the only way He will move upon the face of your situation is when He receives the Word from the Lord. The only way to see lasting victory in your life is to stand on the Word of God. The Holy Spirit always responds to God's Word. God cannot deny Himself. He is God the Father, God the Son (who is the Word), and God the Holy Spirit.

There is a story[3] on syndicated radio about a mighty captain who sailed the high seas for years. He was a captain of an aircraft carrier and played a part in winning many wars over the years. One night, sailing the high seas, he saw something pop up on the radar. It was headed straight for the ship. The mighty captain yelled into the radio, "Change your course. I'm the captain of this aircraft carrier and you must change your course." The other person responded, "But I can't Captain." The Captain furiously responded, "I am the captain of this great aircraft carrier and you must change your course." The other man replied, "Captain, I can't." By this time the mighty captain was growing angry. He screamed, "I refuse to move my course." The man on the other end of the radio said, "Your choice. I'm a lighthouse!"

God cannot change His Word; it is settled in heaven. When we refuse to obey the authority of God's Word, there are certain consequences that cannot change. Just like that lighthouse God's Word is set and unmoving. The choice is yours! The consequences of a life apart from God's Word is like this captain who was too stubborn to change his course.

"EVEN THE SON OF GOD"

Matthew 3:16-4:11says, "And Jesus, when he was baptized, went up straightway out of the water: and lo, the heavens were opened unto him and he saw the Spirit of God descending like a dove, and lighting upon him: And lo a voice from heaven saying, **This is my beloved Son, in whom I am well pleased.** Then was Jesus led up of the Spirit into the wilderness to be tempted of the devil. And when he had fasted forty days and forty nights, he was afterward an hungered. And when the tempter came to him, he said, **If thou be the Son of God, command that these stones be made bread.** But He answered and said, It is written, Man shall not live by bread alone, but by every word that proceedeth out of the mouth of God. Then the devil taketh him up into the holy city, and setteth him on a pinnacle of the temple, And saith unto him, *IF THOU BE THE SON OF GOD*, cast thyself down:

for it is written He shall give his angels charge concerning thee: and in their hands they shall bear thee up, lest at anytime thou dash thy foot against a stone. Jesus said unto him, It is written again Thou shalt not tempt the Lord thy God. Again the devil taketh him up into an exceeding high mountain, and sheweth him all the kingdom's of the world, and the glory of them; And saith unto him, all these things will I give thee, if thou wilt fall down and worship me. Then saith Jesus unto him, Get thee hence, Satan: for it is written, Thou shalt worship the Lord thy God, and him only shalt thou serve. Then the devil leaveth him, and, behold, angels came and ministered unto him."

Even the Son of God was tempted by Satan to operate outside the Word of God. At the end of Matthew 3, the Word of God came from heaven, declaring Jesus as the Son of God. Immediately after the Word came, Jesus was tempted on that Word. Mark 4:4 says Satan comes as soon as the Word is sown, to steal that Word. The Word was "This is my beloved Son," but Satan came immediately and said, "If thou be the Son of God, command these stones to be made bread."

Satan tempted Jesus to operate outside God's Word. Jesus didn't react to His situation. He didn't "get in the flesh" and forget who He was. He didn't get caught up in His circumstances. Jesus stood on the written Word of God, declared, and decreed the Word of the Lord into His situation. "It is written" echoed throughout all the wilderness as Jesus declared Deuteronomy 8:3 in the midst of his trial.

One thing you must understand is that it is not enough to just decree and declare the Word of God. You **must** mix your faith with that Word. Satan didn't take off running the first time. He came again and said, "If thou be the Son of God," but this time he tried to pervert the Word of God. Satan quoted Psalms 91:11-12, but he omitted a very important part of verse 11. The reason angels were released was to "keep thee in all thy ways." Whose ways? God's ways. How do you know God's ways? **God's Word is God's ways!** If you are outside God's way, you are outside His Word, and that's exactly what Satan tried to get Jesus to do.

Jesus was not moved outside the authority of God's Word. Jesus said, "It is written, Thou shalt not tempt the Lord thy God." Once again Jesus used the Word to smash against the plan of Satan, but Satan still didn't give up. Satan offered Jesus all the kingdoms of the world, but Jesus stood on the written word (which is logos in Greek). He declared, "It is written," once more, and Jesus remembered the spoken Word (which is rhema in Greek) that declared Jesus as the Son of God. After three attacks Satan left for a season.

Faith is the substance of things hoped for, and the evidence of things not yet seen (Hebrews 11:1). When we are standing on God's Word, the manifestation of that Word doesn't happen instantly. God wants to see your faith mixed with His Word. That means there will be times when your situation and God's Word about your situation will not match up. The victory comes when your faith in God's Word is greater than your faith in your situation.

From the beginning of time, beyond the beginning, and even in your life right now, Satan's plan is to discredit and disprove God's Word. Why does he fight the Word of God so hard? Because Satan knows once you step out into the realm of faith in God's Word, he is a defeated foe! When you start believing and obeying the Word of God, the supernatural is released in your life.

In Luke's account of Jesus' temptation, we find right after Satan departed for a season that the supernatural was released into Jesus' life even greater than before. This is where God wants you as His child. He wants you to have a lifestyle of victory.

Luke 4:13-21 states, "And when the devil had ended all the temptation, he departed for a season. And Jesus returned in the power of the spirit into Galilee: and there went out a fame of him through all the region round about. And he taught in their synagogues, being glorified of all. And he came to Nazareth, where he had been brought up: and, as his custom was, he went into the synagogue on the Sabbath day, and stood up for to read. And there was delivered unto him the book of the prophet Isaiah. And when he had opened the book, he found the place where it was written. The Spirit of the Lord is upon me, because he hath anointed me to preach the gospel to the poor; he hath sent me to heal the brokenhearted, to preach deliverance to the captives, and recovering of sight to the blind, to set at liberty them that are bruised, to preach the acceptable year of the Lord. And he closed the book, and he gave it again to the minister, and sat down. And the eyes of all them that were in the synagogue were fastened on him. And he began to say unto them, This day is this scripture fulfilled in your ears."

Understand, Jesus just came out of his wilderness experience where the Word of the Lord was tested in Jesus' life concerning whether or not He was truly the Son of God. After Jesus passed this test, He "returned in the power of the Spirit." Once He returned in the power of the Holy Spirit, He was able to enter into His own hometown around all the people he grew up with and proclaim He was the Messiah. Everybody was watching him. His family, His friends, and even the Rabbis who had taught Jesus the Word of God were watching. Imagine the criticism He received. "Jesus has really lost his mind. I remember when I changed His diapers. And now, look at Him. He thinks He is God!" I can hear the priests now, "I remember when I taught him to read the Torah. All this education has gone to his head." We have no idea what Jesus had to go through that day, but we do know that He went through it in victory.

Notice, Satan never tempted Jesus in this area again. Once Jesus received the victory, He remained victorious. Jesus came as our example. Why was Jesus anointed with the Holy Spirit and then tested? Why didn't Jesus go straight into ministry? Jesus won his battles with the Word. He was our example. He allowed us to see that everyone, even the Son of God, goes through a period of the Word being tested in their lives. A child doesn't go from sixth grade straight into the tenth grade. He has to pass each grade. If the school system of America passed out diplomas in the sixth grade and did not allow our nation's children to learn and grow in wisdom, our nation would be in worse shape than we are today.

All truth is parallel. Whatever happens in the Spirit also happens in the natural. We must pass the spiritual test in order to pass to the next grade. The only way to pass is to stand on the Word of God. We serve an infinite God who has no end. He will give you as much of Himself as you will let Him (Matthew 5:6).

The only way to walk in a victorious Christian lifestyle is to stay in the authority and power of God's Word through Jesus Christ. Don't be moved by your circumstances or what you see. Learn to stand on the Word of God and see the salvation of the Lord.

Jeremiah 29:11 says, "For I know the thoughts that I think toward you, saith the Lord, thoughts of peace, and not of evil, to give you an expected end." Start believing what God's Word says about you and your situation. Stop believing the lies that Satan has fed man from the beginning of time. The reason Satan attacks the Word is because he knows if you war without the Word you can not win. When you start to put your faith in Jesus Christ and His Word, the supernatural will happen in your life. Don't take my word for it; try it for yourself.

Notes:
[1]Strong, James (1990). *The New Strong's Exhaustive Concordance of the Bible*. Nashville, TN: Thomas Nelson, Inc. râ'âh (#7200) Hebrew.
[2]Strong, James (1990). *The New Strong's Exahaustive Concordance of the Bible*. Nashville, TN: Thomas Nelson, Inc. diakrinō (#1252) Greek.
[3]This syndicated radio story is taken from Life Line Productions located in Santa Rosa, California.

Shawn Patrick Williams

CHAPTER FOUR

WARRING IN A
PLACE OF REST

The first year that I was the pastor of a small church in Greenwood, South Carolina, God started to burden me for a change in my city. So moved by this conviction was I that I started to talk with other pastors, intercessors, and spiritual leaders in my community. In the past, I had seen how well churches in the city could pull together for evangelistic meetings and things of that nature; however, after these meetings would end, so did the power of the unity between churches in our city.

After much prayer, meetings with my Bishop, meetings with a leader of a nationally known prayer organization, and other leaders in the city, a group of leaders decided to start a citywide intercessory prayer group. We met and all agreed on a place and date for our first meeting. We prayed and decided to concentrate on specific areas to target for our city and region. A few days prior to this event, it seemed like everything in the world that could go wrong, did go wrong.

My home seemed to become a spiritual bulls-eye for the army of Hell. The atmosphere was almost unbearable! My wife and I were in our first year of marriage, fresh in the ministry, and we were not ready for the heavy demonic attacks. God actually gave us a vision of angels dressed in WWII soldier's uniforms to symbolize the spiritual atmosphere we were in. We went through the first meeting with great success. It was a powerful meeting, and as a whole, we saw a lot of breakthrough in the churches that participated.

A few days later after the first meeting, guess what? The personal spiritual attacks were worse than in the days before the meeting. I couldn't understand why I wasn't seeing the victory in spiritual warfare as I did when I broke away from the occultic network. The prayer network continued to have meetings and did see a lot of awesome things happen. Racial prejudices were broken and healed. Healings between clergy and laymen took place, and even a 40-year-old split of a participating church was healed around the same time. But the personal attacks were taking a toll on my family.

After a year of intensive prayer, we felt led to stop having these city-wide prayer meetings for a while. I needed to regroup and seek the Lord concerning why there was so much spiritual backlash that we seemed not to have the victory over. I began to study God's Word, fast, and pray for the explanation to the defeat we had encountered. Several months later, as I was in the Word, God showed me I was ***warring in the wrong place!***

In 2 Chronicles 20:1-30, there is a story of King Jehoshaphat, King of Judah. The Moabites and Ammonites, who were both descendants of Lot, came against Jehoshaphat to battle. Verse 2 states there was "a great multitude" coming against Judah. Jehoshaphat grew afraid because he knew there was no chance for him to win this battle. He proclaimed a fast throughout all of Judah and started to seek God for help. Jehoshaphat went to the house of God and stood in the congregation and started to make a proclamation to the Lord.

As I started to read this part of the story, God spoke to me and said, "Jehoshaphat was warring from the right place." God began to show me how I was warring in the wrong place. As you get into this fabulous story of victory, you find the Spirit of God came into the midst of the congregation where Jehoshaphat was standing, and Jaha'ziel began to prophesy. "For the battle is not yours, but God's. Ye shall not need to fight in this battle: set yourselves, stand ye still, and see the salvation of the Lord with you, O Judah and Jerusalem: fear not, nor be dismayed; tomorrow go out against them: for the Lord will be with you" (2 Chronicles 20:15-17). By the time Jehoshaphat and Judah came to fight, the Ammonites and Moabites had already killed each other and all Judah had to do was "take away the spoil." When you get to the end of the story in verse 30, it says, "So the realm of Jehoshaphat was quiet: for his God gave him rest round about."

There is one fact in spiritual warfare that you must never, never forget! Satan has already been defeated! God wants all His children to have rest around about. The problem comes when you try to war in your own strength. The battle was never meant for you to fight in the first place. The reason Jehoshaphat stood in this place of rest was because he stood on the Word of God. Jehoshaphat didn't just stand up in the middle of the congregation of Judah and beg God for mercy. Jehoshaphat patterned his prayer on the scripture. Hundreds of years before, King David prayed a very similar prayer like the one Jehoshaphat prayed, and the glory of God fell in the temple at the end of the prayer. As the King of Judah, Jehoshaphat studied the scriptures to understand the successes of his ancestors. He knew what the Word said and he stood on it.

The reason I experienced such a spiritual attack during the year we formed the prayer network was because I was warring in the wrong place. Somewhere from my salvation and my experience of leaving the occult, I had forgotten how to stand on God's Word for victory. I had gone from warring in the place of God's authority and God's power, to trying to fight in my own power. And I was losing!

When you step outside the boundaries of God's Word, you get off balance. Just shouting at the devil won't cut it. I think fasting, prayer walks, binding and loosening, and all these things are all good things when it comes to spiritual warfare. However, when they are done aside from the authority and power of the Word of God, they will lead you into a cycle I call the *Deadly Ds*.

When you war without the Word you will be **D**iscouraged because the warfare will not be effective. Warring without the Word is like going to a sword fight with only a shield. The only thing you can do is protect yourself with the shield of faith defensively. There is no offensive weapon, and after a while you will become worn down and ultimately defeated. Let me share with you a story about discouragement a dear friend shared with me.

In the realm of the spirit world, there was a demon named Robok searching for a weapon of destruction that he might thwart the work of God. He searched deep in the world of wickedness until he came to the shop of Satan. There stood Satan to welcome his new slave, and the slave beheld all the tools of havoc that were used to destroy the souls of men. Robok saw the tool of hate with its sharp edges and long stinger. He also saw the tool of temptation with its ropes of lust, which were used to deceive the minds of men. Robok saw all the tools with their prices and powers with them. Yet behind the chief demon himself was a long sleek dark tool which was more expensive than all the others were. It seemed to hang with pride high above the rest. Satan said in a sinister voice, "This is the tool of discouragement, and if we can drive the poison thereof into a man's soul, we can rule his heart and mind and control him with all the other tools we have!" My dear friend, you can't afford to be discouraged!

Secondly, when you war without the Word you will become *Doubtful*. After discouragement sets in, you begin to doubt God and His abilities in your life. Thirdly, once doubt has set in and taken root, you shift into *Depression*. Meditating on depression leads only to one thing, and that is number four. Each phase of this cycle of the *Deadly Ds* sets you up for *Defeat*. This is where Satan wants you, and if you battle him any other way than Warring with the Word, eventually this is where you will end.

Ephesians 6: 10-17 is perhaps the most popular scripture known when it comes to spiritual warfare. Most people get their focus on the hierarchy of angels or the weapons of our warfare, and then they skip the most important part. Verse 10 says, "Finally, my brethren, be strong in the Lord, and <u>in</u> the power of his might." This word interpreted in Greek literally means *to be all the way in, closed up, like in an envelope sealed tightly.* When you step out of the realm of God's Word, you step out of His might.

Spiritual warfare is supposed to be a display of God's might and God's power, not yours! You aren't supposed to do the warfare. You can be in the middle of war experiencing complete rest because you are sealed tightly all the way in Jesus Christ. This kind of warfare is lasting and victorious because Jesus is doing it for you. All you have to do is have faith that the war has already been won, proclaim your victory, and "gather the spoil."

Paul tells us about this place of rest in Hebrews 4:1-2. "Let us therefore fear, lest, a promise being left us of entering into his rest, any of you should seem to come short of it." Paul is saying that it is possible for you to come short of this rest. "For unto us was the gospel preached, as well as unto them: but the word preached did not profit them, not being mixed with faith in them that heard it." Why couldn't some of the Israelites enter into this rest? They found no rest because they did not have faith in God's Word.

Hebrews 4:3-4 says, "For we which have believed do enter into rest, as he said, as I have sworn in my wrath, if they shall enter into my rest: although the works were finished from the foundation of the world." Praise God! The works of our warfare have been finished since the "foundation of the world"! Satan was defeated from the very beginning. "For he spake in a certain place of the seventh day on this wise, And God did rest the seventh day from all his works. And in this place again, If they shall enter into my rest. Seeing therefore it remaineth that some must enter therein, and they to whom it was first preached entered not in because of unbelief." The Greek word for *place* in this scripture is *tŏpŏs²*, and it literally means *a position or spot of opportunity, a condition.* Not everybody wars from a place of rest, because not everybody positions themselves on God's Word when they war. There is a certain position or spot you must stand on to war in a place of rest, and that condition is faith in God's Word.

Satan tried to entice Jesus (the ultimate warrior) to war without the Word, he tempted Michael (the warring angel) in the same way, he did it to me in the prayer network, and he will treat you no differently. He knows that the only way to defeat you is to get you to engage in warfare without the Word. Months went by and this powerful revelation of warring with God's Word started to stir something in my spirit. I started to see such a level of victory in my Christian life like never before. I became so burdened for all the people who would accept Jesus as their Lord and Savior, then their fire would fade away in a few months. Finally, I knew why Satan would try to defeat people early in their Christian life!

The words of that great theologian Billy Mayo would ring in my ears, "The Christian life isn't a 100 yard dash, but a cross-country race." Endurance is key! Through this burden, Warrior Nations International Ministries was born. The motto for WNIM is "winning the war with the Word," based on 2 Corinthians 10:3-5. "For though we walk in the flesh, we do not walk after the flesh: for the weapons of our warfare are not carnal, but mighty through God to the pulling down of strongholds; casting down imaginations, and every high thing that exalteth itself against the knowledge of God, (which is God's Word) and bringing into captivity every thought to the obedience of Christ." One way WNIM carries out this vision is through our *Warring with the Word Conferences*. These conferences are designed to equip, empower, and release the believer into a victorious Christian lifestyle.

When the believer has this revelation as a foundation in his/her journey with Christ, a long lasting, victorious relationship with Christ is found. God wants you winning in life! He has given you the blueprint for victory in His Word.

Pray this prayer with me. Dear God, I repent for ever doubting your Word. I believe it is alive and by my faith in your Word, I will live a life of faith in victory. Holy Spirit, empower me to live for your purposes. Empower me to be a warrior for your kingdom. In the holy and matchless name of Jesus Christ, Amen!

Notes:
[1]Oral Tradition from Kenneth Washington from July 23, 2003.
[2]Strong, James (1990). *The New Strong's Exhaustive Concordance of the Bible.* Nashville, TN: Thomas Nelson, Inc. tŏpŏs (#5117) Greek.

CHAPTER FIVE

AMMO FOR ENGAGEMENT
A USER'S GUIDE

The Bible has over 47,000 promises that God gave to His children. No matter what happens to you during your life, the answer is found in God's Word. Whatever the battle may be, the key to your being victorious is in the Bible.

This book of selected scriptures is compiled for your quick reference when you need ammo in a particular situation. This book is in no way meant to replace your regular Bible reading or to be used for in-depth studies on a particular subject. Just as vitamins aren't designed to replace regular meals, but rather enhance your normal intake of food, so is this book to the Believer. There are many topics in life this book doesn't cover.

Over 80 of life's topics are available to you here. If you're looking for a quick Word from the Word to give you strength, you will find it here.

All scriptures are taken from The King James Version of the Bible. All topics are arranged in alphabetical order.

<u>Anorexia</u>
<u>I Corinthians 3:16-17</u> "Know ye not that ye are the temple of God, and that the Spirit of God dwelleth in you? If any man defile the temple of God, him shall God destroy; for the temple of God is holy, which temple ye are."

<u>I Corinthians 6:19-7:2</u> "What? Know ye not that your body is the temple of the Holy Ghost which is in you, which ye have of God, and ye are not your own? For ye are brought with a price: therefore glorify God in your body, and in your spirit, which are God's.

<u>James 5:14-16</u> "Is any sick among you? Let him call for the elders of the church; and let them pray over him anointing him with oil in the name of the Lord: And the prayer of faith shall save the sick, and the Lord shall raise him up; and if he have committed sins, they shall be forgiven him. Confess your faults one to another, and pray one for another, that ye may be healed. The effectual fervent prayer of a righteous man availeth much."

<u>I Peter 2:24</u> Who his own self bare our sins in his own body on the tree, that we, being dead to sins, should live unto righteousness: by whose stripes ye were healed."

Jeremiah 17:14 "Heal me, O Lord, and I shall be healed; save me, and I shall be saved: for thou art my praise."

Jeremiah 30:17 "For I will restore health unto thee, and I will heal thee of thy wounds, saith the Lord."

Romans 8:12-13 "Therefore, brethren, we are debtors, not to the flesh to live after the flesh. For if ye live after the flesh, ye shall die: but if ye through the Spirit do mortify the deeds of the body, ye shall live."

Anger

Proverbs 15:18 "A wrathful man stirreth up strife: but he that is slow to anger appeaseth strife."

Colossians 3:8 "But now ye also put off all these: anger, wrath, malice, blasphemy, filthy communication out of your mouth."

Proverbs 15:1 "A soft answer turneth away wrath; but grievous words stir up anger."

Ephesians 4:26 "Be ye angry, and sin not; let not the sun go down upon your wrath."

Proverbs 19:11 "The discretion of a man deferreth his anger; and it is his glory to pass over a transgression.

<u>Psalm 37:8</u> "Cease from anger, and forsake wrath: fret not thyself in any wise to do evil."

<u>Matthew 5:22</u> "But I say unto you, that whosoever is angry with his brother without a cause shall be in danger of the judgment."

<u>Ecclesiastes 7:9</u> "Be not hasty in thy spirit to be angry: for anger resteth in the bosom of fools."

<u>Nehemiah 9:17</u> "A God ready to pardon, gracious and merciful, slow to anger, and of great kindness.."

<u>Proverbs 21:19</u> "It is better to dwell in the wilderness, than with a contentious and an angry woman."

<u>Colossians 3:21</u> "Fathers, provoke not your children to anger, lest they be discouraged."

<u>Proverbs 29:22</u> "An angry man stirreth up strife, and a furious man aboundeth in transgression."

<u>Psalm 30:5</u> "For his anger endureth but a moment; in his favor is life: weeping may endure for a night, but joy cometh in the morning."

<u>Ephesians 4:31-32</u> "Let all bitterness, and wrath, and anger, and clamor, and evil speaking, be put away

from you with all malice: And be ye kind one to another, tenderhearted, forgiving one another, even as God for Christ's sake hath forgiven you."

Proverbs 27:4 "Wrath is cruel, and anger is outrageous: but who is able to stand before envy?"

Proverbs 22:24-25 "Make no friendship with an angry man; and with a furious man thou shalt not go: lest thou learn his ways, and get a snare to thy soul."

Anxiety

Mark 4:18-19 "And these are they which are sown among thorns; such as hear the word. And the cares of this world, the deceitfulness of riches, and the lusts of other things entering in, choke the word, and it becometh unfruitful."

Philippians 4:6 "Be careful for nothing; but in everything by prayer and supplication with thanksgiving let your requests be made known unto God."

Psalm 32:7 "Thou art my hiding place; thou shalt preserve me from trouble; thou shalt compass me about with songs of deliverance."

Romans 8:28 "And we know that all things work together for good to them that love God, to them who are the called according to his purpose."

Matthew 6:31-33 "Therefore take no thought, saying, What shall we eat? Or, What shall we drink? Or, Where withal shall we be clothed? (For after all these things do the Gentiles seek:) for your heavenly Father knoweth that ye have need of all these things. But seek ye first the kingdom of God, and his righteousness; and all these things shall be added unto you.

Psalm 9:9-10 "The Lord also will be a refuge for the oppressed, a refuge in times of trouble. And they that know thy name will put their trust in thee; for thou, Lord, hast not forsaken them that seek thee."

Luke 10:41-42 "And Jesus answered and said unto her, Martha, Martha, thou art careful and troubled about many things: But one thing is needful: and Mary hath chosen that good part, which shall not be taken away from her."

Authority of the Believer
I John 4:4 "Ye are of God, little children, and have overcome them: because greater is he that is in you, than he that is in the world."

Matthew 16:19 "And I will give unto thee the keys of the kingdom of heaven: and whatsoever thou shalt bind on earth shall be bound in heaven: and whatsoever thou shalt loose on earth shall be loosed in heaven."

Ephesians 3:20 "Now unto him that is able to do exceedingly abundantly above all that we ask or think, according to the power that worketh in us,"

I John 5:4 "For whatsoever is born of God overcometh the world: and this is the victory that overcometh the world, even our faith.

John 17:20-21 "Neither pray I for these alone, but for them also which shall believe on me through their word; That they all may be one; as thou, Father, art in me, and I in thee, that they also may be one in us: that the world may believe that thou hast sent me."

Acts 5:32 "And we are his witnesses of these things; and so is also the Holy Ghost, whom God hath given to them that obey him."

Matthew 28:18-20 "And Jesus came and spake unto them, saying, All power is given unto me in heaven and in earth. Go ye therefore, and teach all nations, baptizing them in the name of the Father, and of the

Son, and of the Holy Ghost: Teaching them to observe all things whatsoever I have commanded you: and lo, I am with you always, even unto the end of the world."

John 15:7 "If ye abide in me, and my words abide in you, ye shall ask what ye will, and it shall be done unto you."

John 1:12 "But as many as received him, to them gave he power to become the sons of God, even to them that believe on his name."

Belief
John 12:46 "I am come a light into the world, that whosoever believeth on me should not abide in darkness."

John 6:47 "Verily, verily, I say unto you, he that believeth on me hath everlasting life."

John 20:29 "Jesus saith unto him, Thomas, because thou hast seen me, thou hast believed: blessed are they that have not seen, and yet have believed."

John 3:16 "For God so loved the world, that he gave his only begotten Son, that whosoever believeth in him should not perish, but have everlasting life."

<u>Mark 9:23</u> "Jesus said unto him, If thou canst believe, all things are possible to him that believeth."

<u>John 6:35</u> "And Jesus said unto them, I am the bread of life: he that cometh to me shall never hunger; and he that believeth on me shall never thirst."

<u>Acts 16:31</u> "And they said, Believe on the Lord Jesus Christ, and thou shalt be saved, and thy house."

<u>I Peter 2:6</u> "Wherefore also it is contained in the scripture, Behold, I lay in Sion a chief cornerstone, elect, precious: and he that believeth on him shall not be confounded."

<u>John 3:36</u> "He that believeth on the Son hath everlasting life: and he that believeth not the Son shall not see life; but the wrath of God abideth on him."

<u>John 1:12</u> "But as many as received him, to them gave he power to become the sons of God, even to them that believe on his name."

Bitterness
<u>Proverbs 14:10</u> "The heart knoweth his own bitterness; and a stranger doth not intermeddle with his joy."

<u>Proverbs 17:25</u> "A foolish son is a grief to his father, and bitterness to her that bare him."

<u>Isaiah 38:15-16</u> "What shall I say? He hath both spoken unto me, and himself hath done it: I shall go softly all my years in the bitterness of my soul. O, Lord, by these things men live, and in all these things is the life of my spirit: so wilt thou recover me, and make me to live."

<u>Acts 8:22-23</u> "Repent therefore of this wickedness, and pray God, if perhaps the thought of thine heart may be forgiven thee. For I perceive that thou art in the gall of bitterness, and in the bond of iniquity."

<u>Ephesians 4:31-32</u> "Let all bitterness, and wrath, and anger, and clamour, and evil speaking, be put away from you, with all malice: And be ye kind one to another, tender hearted, forgiving one another, even as God for Christ's sake hath forgiven you."

<u>Hebrews 12:14-15</u> "Follow peace with all men, and holiness, without which no man shall see the Lord: Looking diligently lest any man fail of the grace of God; lest any root of bitterness springing up trouble you, and thereby many be defiled:"

Bondage

Romans 8:15 "For ye have not received the spirit of bondage again to fear: but ye have received the Spirit of adoption, whereby we cry, Abba, Father."

Galatians 5:1 "Stand fast therefore in the liberty where with Christ hath made us free, and be not entangled again with the yoke of bondage."

II Thessalonians 2:13 "But we are bound to give thanks always to God for you, brethren beloved of the Lord, because God hath from the beginning chosen you to salvation through sanctification of the Spirit and belief of the truth:"

2 Corinthians 5:17 "Therefore if any man be in Christ, he is a new creature: old things are passed away; behold, all things are become new."

Romans 6:14 "For sin shall not have dominion over you: for ye are not under the law, but under grace."

Galatians 4:3-5 "Even so we, when we where children, were in bondage under the elements of the world: but when the fullness of time was come, God sent forth his Son, made of a woman, made under the law, to redeem them that were under the law, that we might receive the adoption of sons."

<u>Colossians 3:10-11</u> "And have put on the new man, which is renewed in knowledge after the image of him that created him: Where there is neither Greek nor Jew, circumcision nor uncircumcision, Barbarian, Scythian, bond nor free: but Christ is all, and in all."

<u>Psalm 146:7</u> "Which executeth judgment for the oppressed: which giveth food to the hungry. The Lord looseth the prisoners."

Business Matters
<u>Proverbs 11:15</u> "He that is surety for a stranger shall smart for it, and he that hateth suretyship is sure."

<u>Proverbs 10:3-4</u> "The Lord will not suffer the soul of the righteous to famish: but he casteth away the substance of the wicked. He becometh poor that dealeth with a slack hand: but the hand of the diligent maketh rich."

<u>Proverbs 3:27</u> "Withhold not good from them to whom it is due; when it is in the power of thine hand to do it."

<u>Proverbs 17:23</u> "A wicked man taketh a gift out of the bosom to pervert the ways of judgment."

<u>Proverbs 11:1</u> "A false balance is an abomination to the Lord: but a just weight is his delight."

Proverbs 27:23-24 "Be thou diligent to know the state of thy flocks, and look well to thy herds. For riches are not forever: and doth the crown endure to every generation?"

Proverbs 14:23 "In all labour there is profit: but the talk of the lips tendeth only to penury."

Romans 12:11 "Not slothful in business; fervent in Spirit; serving the Lord."

Proverbs 28:19 "He that tilleth his land shall have plenty of bread: but he that followeth after vain persons shall have poverty enough."

Proverbs 20:13 "Love not sleep, lest thou come to poverty; open thine eyes, and thou shalt be satisfied with bread."

Proverbs 12:24 "The hand of the diligent shall bear rule; but the slothful shall be under tribute."

Children
Proverbs 17:6 "Children's children are the crown of old men; and the glory of children are their fathers."

Psalm 127:3-5 "Lo, children are an heritage of the Lord: and the fruit of the womb is his reward. As arrows are in the hand of a mighty man; so are children of the youth. Happy is the man that hath his quiver full of them: they shall not be ashamed, but they shall speak with the enemies in the gate."

Isaiah 54:13 "And all thy children shall be taught of the Lord, and great shall be the peace of thy children."

Isaiah 44:3 "For I will pour water upon him that is thirsty, and floods upon the dry ground: I will pour my spirit upon thy seed, and my blessing upon thine offspring."

Matthew 18:5 "And whoso shall receive one such little child in my name receiveth me."

Acts 2:39 "For the promise is unto you, and to your children, and to all that are afar off, even as many as the Lord our God shall call."

Acts 16:31 "And they said, Believe on the Lord Jesus Christ, and thou shalt be saved, and thy house."

Matthew 19:14 "But Jesus said, Suffer little children, and forbid them not, to come unto me: for of such is the kingdom of heaven."

Ecclesiastes 12:1 "Remember now thy Creator in the days of thy youth, while the evil days come not, nor the years draw nigh, when thou shalt say, I have no pleasure in them;"

Children's Instruction

Ephesians 6:1-3 "Children, obey your parents in the Lord: for this is right. Honour thy father and mother; which is the first commandment with promise; That it may be well with thee, and thou mayest live long on the earth."

Proverbs 8:32-33 "Now therefore hearken unto me, O ye children: for blessed are they that keep my ways. Hear instruction, and be wise, and refuse it not."

Colossians 3:20 "Children, obey your parents in all things: for this is well pleasing unto the Lord."

Proverbs 22:6 "Train up a child in the way he should go: and when he is old, he will not depart from it."

Proverbs 1:10 "My Son, if sinners entice thee, consent thou not."

Luke 18:20 "…Honour thy father and thy mother."

Proverbs 23:22 "Hearken unto thy father that begat thee, and despise not thy mother when she is old."

Proverbs 20:11 "Even a child is known by his doings, whether his work be pure, and whether it be right."

Proverbs 10:1 "...A wise son maketh a glad father: but a foolish son is the heaviness of his mother."

Leviticus 19:3 "Ye shall fear every man his mother, and his father..."

Deuteronomy 27:16 "Cursed be he that setteth light by his father or his mother..."

Comfort

Psalm 23:4 "Yea, though I walk through the valley of the shadow of death, I will fear no evil: for thou art with me; thy rod and thy staff they comfort me."

Matthew 11:28 "Come unto me, all ye that are heavy laden, and I will give you rest."

Psalm 55:22 "Cast thy burden upon the Lord, and he shall sustain thee: he shall never suffer the righteous to be moved."

Matthew 9:22 "But Jesus turned him about, and when he saw her, he said, Daughter, be of good comfort; thy faith hath made thee whole, And the woman was made whole from that hour."

2 Corinthians 1:3-4 "Blessed be God, even the Father of our Lord Jesus Christ, the Father of mercies, and the God of all comfort; Who comforteth us in all our tribulation, that we may be able to comfort them which are in any trouble, by the comfort wherewith we ourselves are comforted of God."

Philippians 2:1-2 "If there be therefore any consolation in Christ, if any comfort of love, if any fellowship of the Spirit, if any bowels and mercies, Fulfill ye my joy, that ye be likeminded, having the same love, being of one accord, of one mind."

Psalm 9:9 "The Lord also will be a refuge for the oppressed, a refuge in times of trouble."

John 16:33 "These things I have spoken unto you, that in me ye might have peace. In the world ye shall have tribulation: but be of good cheer; I have overcome the world."

Psalm 27:14 "Wait on the Lord: be of good courage, and he shall strengthen thine heart: wait, I say, on the Lord."

Compassion

<u>Psalm 78:38-39</u> "But he, being full of compassion, forgave their iniquity, and destroyed them not: yea, many a time turned he his anger away, and did not stir up all his wrath. For he remembered that they were but flesh; a wind that passeth away, and cometh not again."

<u>Lamentations 3:22</u> "It is of the Lord's mercies that we are not consumed, because his compassions fail not."

<u>Matthew 15:32</u> "Then Jesus called his disciples unto him, and said, I have compassion on the multitude, because they continue with me now three days, and have nothing to eat: and I will not send them away fasting, lest they faint in the way."

<u>Mark 1:40-41</u> "And there came a leper to him, beseeching him, and kneeling down to him, and saying unto him, If thou wilt, thou canst make me clean. And Jesus, moved with compassion, put forth his hand, and touched him, and saith unto him, I will; be thou clean."

<u>I Peter 3:8-9</u> "Finally, be ye all of one mind, having compassion one of another, love as brethren, be pitiful, be courteous: Not rendering evil for evil, or railing for railing but contrariwise blessing: knowing that ye are thereunto called, that ye should inherit a blessing."

<u>I John 3:17</u> "But whoso hath this world's good, and seeth his brother have need, and shutteth up his bowels of compassion from him, how dwelleth the love of God in him?"

<u>Confession</u>

<u>Proverbs 18:20-21</u> "A man's belly shall be satisfied with the fruit of his mouth, and with the increase of his lips shall he be filled. Death and life are in the power of the tongue: and they that love it shall eat the fruit thereof."

<u>Proverbs 18:4</u> "The words of a man's mouth are as deep waters, and the wellspring of wisdom as a flowing brook."

<u>Romans 10:8-10</u> "But what saith it? The word is nigh thee, even in thy mouth, and in thy heart: that is, the word of faith which we preach: That if thou shalt confess with thy mouth the Lord Jesus, and shalt believe in thine heart that God hath raised him from the dead, thou shalt be saved."

<u>Mark 11:22-24</u> "And Jesus answering saith unto them, Have faith in God. For verily I say unto you, that whosoever shall say unto this mountain, Be thou removed, and be thou cast into the sea; and shall not doubt in his heart, but shall believe that those things which he saith shall come to pass; he shall have

whatsoever he saith. Therefore I say unto you, what things soever ye desire, when ye pray, believe that ye receive them, and ye shall have them."

James 5:16 "Confess your faults one to another, and pray one for another, that ye may be healed. The effectual fervent prayer of a righteous man availeth much."

Hebrews 11:3 "Through faith we understand that the worlds were framed by the word of God, so that things which are seen were not made of things which do appear."

Correction
Proverbs 3:12 "For whom the Lord loveth he correcteth; even as a father the son in whom he delighteth."

I Corinthians 11:32 "But when we are judged, we are chastened of the Lord, that we should not be condemned with the world."

Hebrews 12:10-11 "For they verily for a few days chastened us after their own pleasure; but he for our profit, that we might be partakers of his holiness. Now no chastening for the present seemeth to be joyous, but grievous: nevertheless afterward it yieldeth the peaceable fruit of righteousness unto them which are exercised thereby."

2 Corinthians 4:16-17 "For which cause we faint not; but though our outward man perish, yet the inward man is renewed day by day. For our light affliction, which is but for a moment, worketh for us a far more exceeding and eternal weight of glory."

Psalm 94:12-13 "Blessed is the man whom thou chastenest, O Lord. And teachest him out of thy law; Thou that mayest give him rest from the days of adversity, until the pit be digged for the wicked."

Job 5:17-18 "Behold, happy is the man whom God correcteth: therefore despise not thou the chastening of the Almighty: For he maketh sore, and bindeth up: he woundeth, and his hands make whole."

Proverbs 3:11 "My son, despise no the chastening of the Lord: neither be weary of his correction:"

Covetousness
Hebrews 13:5 "Let your conversation be without covetousness: and be content with such things as ye have: for he hath said, I will never leave thee, nor forsake thee."

Luke 12:15 "And he said unto them take heed, and beware of covetousness: for a man's life consiseth not in the abundance of the things which he possesseth."

Exodus 20:17 "Thou shalt not covet thy neighbour's house, thou shalt not covet thy neighbour's wife, nor his manservant, nor his maidservant, nor his ox, nor his ass, nor anything that is thy neighbour's."

I Corinthians 6:10 "Nor thieves, nor covetous, nor drunkards, nor revilers, nor extortioners, shall inherit the kingdom of God.

I Timothy 3:2-3 "A bishop then must be blameless, the husband of one wife, viligant, sober, of good behavior, given to hospitality, apt to teach; not given to wine, no striker, not greedy of filthy lucre; but patient, not a brawler, not covetous;"
Psalm 119:36 "Incline my heart unto thy testimonies, and not to covetousness."

Ecclesiastes 5:10-11 "He that loveth silver shall not be satisfied with silver; nor he that loveth abundance with increase: this is also vanity. When goods increase, they are increased that eat them: and what good is there to the owners thereof, saving the beholding of them with their eyes?"

Creation

Revelation 4:11 "Thou art worthy, O Lord, to receive glory and honor and power: for thou hast created all things, and for thy pleasure they are and were created."

Colossians 1:12-17 "Giving thanks unto the Father, which hath made us meet to be partakers of the inheritance of the saints in light: Who hath delivered us from the power of darkness, and hath translated us into the kingdom of his dear Son: In whom we have redemption through his blood, even the forgiveness of sins: Who is the image of the invisible God, the firstborn of every creature: For by him were all things created, that are in heaven and that are in earth, visible and invisible, whether they be thrones, or dominions, or principalities, or powers: all things were created by him, and for him: And he is before all things, and by him all things consist."

Hebrews 11:3 "Through faith we understand that the worlds were framed by the word of God, so that things which are seen were not made of things which do appear."

Genesis 1:1-2 "In the beginning God created the heaven and the earth. And the earth was without form, and void; and darkness was upon the face of the deep.

And the Spirit of God moved upon the face of the waters."

<u>Genesis 2:1-2</u> "Thus the heavens and the earth were finished and all the host of them. And on the seventh day God ended his work which he had made; and he rested on the seventh day from all his work which he had made."

<u>Death</u>
<u>2 Corinthians 4:16</u> "…But though our outward man perish, yet the inward man is renewed day by day."

<u>Psalm 49:15</u> "But God will redeem my soul from the power of the grave: for he shall receive me."

<u>Psalm 116:15</u> "Precious in the sight of the Lord is the death of his saints."

<u>Psalm 118:17</u> "I shall not die, but live, and declare the works of the Lord."

<u>Psalm 23:4</u> "Yea, though I walk through the valley of the shadow of death, I will fear no evil: for thou art with me; thy rod and thy staff they comfort me."

<u>Isaiah 25:8</u> "He will swallow up death in victory; and the Lord God will wipe away tears from off all faces..."

<u>I Corinthians 15:55</u> "O death, where is thy sting? O grave, where is thy victory?"

<u>John 8:51</u> "Verily, verily, I say unto you, If a man keep my saying, he shall never see death."

<u>Psalm 48:14</u> "For this God is our God for ever and ever: he will be our guide even unto death."

<u>Hosea 13:14</u> "I will ransom them from the power of the grave; I will redeem them from death: O death, I will be thy plagues; O grave, I will be thy destruction: repentance shall be hid from mine eyes."

<u>John 3:15</u> "That whosoever believeth in him should not perish, but have eternal life."

<u>Doubt</u>

<u>Matthew 21:21</u> "Jesus answered and said unto them, Verily I say unto you, If ye have faith, and doubt not, ye shall not only do this which is done to the fig tree, but also if ye shall say unto this mountain, Be thou removed, and be thou cast into the sea: it shall be done."

<u>Romans 14:22</u> "Hast thou faith? have it to thyself before God. Happy is he that condemneth not himself in that thing which he alloweth. And he that doubteth is damned if he eat, because he eateth not of faith: for whatsoever is not of faith is sin."

<u>Revelation 21:8</u> "But the fearful, and unbelieving, and the abominable, and murderers, and whoremongers, and sorcerers, and idolaters, and all liars, shall have their part in the lake which burneth with fire and brimstone: which is the second death."

<u>Mark 9:23-24</u> "Jesus said unto him, If thou canst believe, all things are possible to him that believeth. And straightway the father of the child cried out, and said with tears, Lord I believe; help thou mine unbelief."

<u>John 20:27-29</u> "Then saith he to Thomas, Reach hither thy finger, and behold my hands; and reach hither thy hand, and thrust it into my side: and be not faithless, but believing. And Thomas answered and said unto him, My Lord and my God. Jesus saith unto him, Thomas, because thou hast seen me, thou hast believed: blessed are they that have not seen, and yet have believed."

2 Corinthians 6:14 "Be ye not unequally yoked together with unbelievers: for what fellowship hath righteousness with unrighteousness? and what communion hath light with darkness?

Enemies

Deuteronomy 28:7 "The Lord shall cause thine enemies that rise up against thee to be smitten before thy face: they shall come out against thee one way, and flee before thee seven ways."

Deuteronomy 20:4 "For the Lord your God is he that goeth with you, to fight for you against your enemies, to save you."

Psalm 60:12 "Through God we shall do valiantly: for he it is that shall tread down our enemies."

Psalm 23:5 "Thou preparest a table before me in the presence of mine enemies: thou anointest my head with oil; my cup runneth over."

Psalm 25: 19-20 "Consider mine enemies; for they are many; and they hate me with cruel hatred. O keep my soul, and deliver me: let me not be ashamed; for I put my trust in thee."

Psalm 27:5-6 "For in the time of trouble he shall hide me in his pavilion: in the secret place of his tabernacle shall he hide me; he shall set me upon a rock. And now shall mine head be lifted up above mine enemies round about me: therefore will I offer in his tabernacle sacrifices of joy; I will sing, yea, I will sing praises unto the Lord."

2 Kings 17:39 "But the Lord your God ye shall fear; and he shall deliver you out of the hand of all your enemies."

Proverbs 16:7 "When a man's ways please the Lord, he maketh even his enemies to be at peace with him."

Psalms 112:8 "His heart is established, he shall not be afraid, until he see his desire upon his enemies."

Envy
Proverbs 23:17 "Let not thine heart envy sinners: but be thou in the fear of the Lord all the day long."

Proverbs 14:30 "A sound heart is the life of the flesh: but envy the rottenness of the bones."

Galatians 5:25-26 "If we live in the Spirit, let us also walk in the Spirit. Let us not be desirous of vain glory, provoking one another, envying one another."

<u>Romans 13:13-14</u>"Let us walk honestly, as in the day; not in rioting and drunkenness, not in chambering and wantonness, not in strife and envying. But put ye on the Lord Jesus Christ, and make not provision for the flesh, to fulfil the lusts thereof."

<u>Titus 3:3-5</u> "For we ourselves also were sometimes foolish, disobedient, deceived, serving divers lusts and pleasures, living in malice and envy, hateful, and hating one another. But after that the kindness and love of God our Savior toward man appeared. Not by works of righteousness which we have done, but according to his mercy he saved us, by the washing of regeneration, and renewing of the Holy Ghost;"

<u>Proverbs 24:1</u> "Be not thou envious against evil men, neither desire to be with them."

<u>Proverbs 3:31</u> "Envy thou not the oppressor, and choose none of his ways."

<u>James 3:16</u> "For where envying and strife is, there is confusion and every evil work."

<u>Psalm 37:7</u> "Rest in the Lord, and wait patiently for him: fret not thyself because of him who prospereth in his way…"

<u>Proverbs 27:4</u> "Wrath is cruel, and anger is outrageous; but who is able to stand before envy?"

<u>I Corinthians 10:24</u> "Let no man seek his own, but every man another's wealth."

Eternal Life

<u>John 3:16</u> "For God so loved the world, that he gave his only begotten Son, that whosoever believeth in him should not perish, but have everlasting life."

<u>Romans 6:23</u> "For the wages of sin is death; but the gift of God is eternal life through Jesus Christ our Lord."

<u>I Corinthians 15:21</u> "For since by man came death, by man came also the resurrection of the dead."

<u>Galatians 6:8</u> "For he that soweth to his flesh shall reap of the flesh corruption; but he that soweth to the Spirit shall of the Spirit reap life everlasting."

<u>I John 5:11</u> "And this is the record, that God hath given to us eternal life, and this life is in his Son."

<u>Romans 8:11</u> "But if the Spirit of him that raised up Jesus from the dead dwell in you, he that raised up

Christ from the dead shall also quicken your mortal bodies by his Spirit that dwelleth in you."

John 6:47 "Verily, verily I say unto you, He that believeth on me hath everlasting life."

John 6:40 "And this is the will of him that sent me, that everyone which seeth the Son, and believeth on him, may have everlasting life: And I will raise him up at the last day."

I John 2:25 "And this is the promise that he hath promised us, even eternal life."

I Thessalonians 4:16 "For the Lord himself shall descend from heaven with a shout, with the voice of the archangel, and with the trump of God: and the dead in Christ shall rise first."

Evangelism

Acts 1:8 "But ye shall receive power, after that the Holy Ghost is come upon you: and ye shall be witnesses unto me both in Jerusalem, and in all Judaea, and in Samaria, and unto the uttermost part of the earth."

Matthew 28:18-20 "And Jesus came and spoke unto them, saying, All power is given unto me in heaven and earth. Go ye therefore, and teach all nations, baptizing them in the name of the Father, and of the Son, and of the Holy Ghost: Teaching them to observe all things whatsoever I have commanded you: and, lo, I am with you always, even unto the end of the world."

Luke 24:46-49 "And said unto them, Thus it is written, and thus it behooved Christ to suffer, and to rise form the dead the third day: And that repentance and remission of sins should be preached in his name among all nations, beginning at Jerusalem. And ye are witnesses of these things. And, behold, I send the promise of my Father upon you: but tarry ye in the city of Jerusalem, until ye be endued with power from on high."

Mark 16:15-18 "And he said unto them, Go ye into all the world, and preach the gospel to every creature. He that believeth and is baptized shall be saved; but he that believeth not shall be damned. And these signs shall follow them that believe; In my name shall they cast out devils; they shall speak with new tongues; They shall take up serpents; and if they drink any deadly thing, it shall not hurt them; they shall lay hands on the sick, and they shall recover."

Faith

Hebrews 11:1 "Now faith is the substance of things hoped for, the evidence of things not seen."

<u>Hebrews 11:6</u> "But without faith it is impossible to please him: for he that cometh to God must believe that he is, and that he is a rewarder of them that diligently seek him."

<u>Galatians 5:22-23</u> "The fruit of the Spirit is love, joy, peace, longsuffering, gentleness, goodness, faith, meekness, temperance: against such there is no law."

<u>2 Corinthians 5:7</u> "For we walk by faith, not by sight."

<u>Ephesians 2:8</u> "For by grace are ye saved through faith and that not of yourselves: it is the gift of God."

<u>Habakkuk 2:4</u> "Behold, his soul which is lifted up is not upright in him: but the just shall live by faith."

<u>Matthew 21:21</u> "Jesus answered and said unto them, Verily I say unto you, If ye have faith, and doubt not, ye shall not only do this which is done to the fig tree, but also if ye shall say unto this mountain, Be thou removed, and be thou cast into the sea; it shall be done."

<u>Romans 10:17</u> "So then faith cometh by hearing, and hearing by the word of God."

James 1:5-6 "If any of you lack wisdom, let him ask of God, that giveth to all men liberally, and upbraideth not; and it shall be given him. But let him ask in faith, nothing wavering. For he that waivereth is like a wave of the sea driven with wind and tossed."

I Corinthians 16:13 "Watch ye, stand fast in the faith, quit you like men, be strong."

Faithfulness of God
Hebrews 10:23 "Let us hold fast the profession of our faith without wavering; (for he is faithful that promised;)"

Psalm 119:89-90 "Forever, O Lord, thy word is settled in heaven. Thy faithfulness is unto all generations…"

2 Corinthians 1:20 "For all the promises of God in him are yea, and in him Amen, unto the glory of God by us."

2 Peter 3:9 "The Lord is not slack concerning his promise, as some men count slackness; but is longsuffering to us-ward…"

Deuteronomy 4:31 "For the Lord thy God is a merciful God; he will not forsake thee, neither destroy thee, nor forget the covenant of thy fathers which he sware unto them."

Psalm 89:34 "My covenant will I not break, nor alter the thing that is gone out of my lips."

Lamentations 3:22-23 "It is of the Lord's mercies that we are not consumed, because his compassions fail not. They are new every morning: great is thy faithfulness."

Psalm 89:1 "I will sing of the mercies of the Lord for ever: with my mouth will I make known thy faithfulness to all generations."

Psalm 92:1-2 "It is a good thing to give thanks unto the Lord, and to sing praises unto thy name, O most High: to shew forth thy lovingkindness in the morning, and thy faithfulness every night."

Isaiah 25:1 "O Lord, thou art my God; I will exalt thee, I will praise thy name; for thou hast done wonderful things; thy counsels of old are faithfulness and truth."

Psalm 9:10 "And they that know thy name will put their trust in thee: for thou, Lord, hast not forsaken them that seek thee."

Failure

Luke 22:32 "But I have prayed for thee, that thy faith fail not; and when thou art converted, strengthen thy brethren."

I Corinthians 13:8 "Charity never faileth: but whether there be prophecies, they shall fail; whether there be tongues, they shall cease; whether there be knowledge it shall vanish away."

Psalm 89:33 "Nevertheless my lovingkindness will I not utterly take from him, nor suffer my faithfulness to fail."

Isaiah 58:11 "And the Lord shall guide thee continually, and satisfy thy soul in drought, and make fat thy bones: and thou shall be like a watered garden, and like a spring of water, whose waters fail not."

Lamentations 3:22 "It is of the Lord's mercies that we are not consumed, because his compassions fail not."

Psalm 37:24 "Though he fall, he shall not be utterly cast down: for the Lord upholdeth him with his hand."

Psalm 73:26 "My flesh and my heart faileth: but God is the strength of my heart, and my portion for ever."

<u>Psalm 34:19</u> "Many are the afflictions of the righteous: but the Lord delivereth him out of them all."

<u>Psalm 9:9</u> "The Lord also will be a refuge for the oppressed, a refuge in times of trouble."

<u>Psalm 138:7</u> "Though I walk in the midst of trouble, thou wilt revive me: thou shalt stretch forth thine hand against the wrath of mine enemies, and thy right hand shall save me."

Favor

<u>Proverbs 3:3-4</u> "Let not mercy and truth forsake thee: bind them about thy neck; write them upon the table of thine heart: So shalt thou find favour and good understanding in the sight of God and man."

<u>Proverbs 8:33-35</u> "Hear instruction, and be wise, and refuse it not. Blessed is the man that heareth me, watching daily at my gates, waiting at the post of my doors. For whoso findeth me findeth life, and shall obtain favour of the Lord."

<u>Proverbs 11:27</u> "He that dilengtly seeketh good procureth favour: but he that seeketh mischief, it shall come unto him."

<u>Proverbs 12:2</u> "A good man obtaineth favour of the Lord: but a man of wicked devices he will condemn."

<u>Proverbs 13:15</u> "Good understanding giveth favour: but the way of the transgressors is hard."

<u>Psalm 5:12</u> "For thou, Lord, wilt bless the righteous; with favour wilt thou compass him as with a shield."

<u>Job 10:12-13</u> "Thou hast granted me life and favour, and thy visitation hath preserved my spirit. And these things hast thou hid in thine heart; I know that this is with thee."

<u>Luke 2:52</u> "And Jesus increased in wisdom and stature, and in favour with God and man."

<u>Proverbs 31:30</u> "Favour is deceitful, and beauty is vain: but a woman that feareth the Lord, she shall be praised."

Fear
<u>2 Timothy 1:7</u> "For God hath not given us the spirit of fear; but of power, and of love, and of a sound mind."

<u>Proverbs 29:25</u> "The fear of man bringeth a snare: but whoso putteth his trust in the Lord shall be safe."

Isaiah 54:4 "Fear not; for thou shalt not be ashamed: neither be thou confounded; for thou shalt not be put to shame..."

Romans 8:15 "For ye have not received the spirit of bondage again to fear; but ye have received the Spirit of adoption, whereby we cry, Abba, Father."

Psalm 23:4 "Yea, though I walk through the valley of the shadow of death, I will fear no evil: for thou art with me; thy rod and thy staff they comfort me."

Proverbs 1:33 "But whoso hearkenth unto me shall dwell safely, and shall be quiet from fear of evil."

Proverbs 3:24 "When thou liest down, thou shalt not be afraid: yea, thou shalt lie down, and thy sleep shall be sweet."

Isaiah 54:14 "In righteousness shalt thou be established: thou shalt be far from oppression; for thou shalt not fear: and from terror; for it shall not come near thee."

Psalm 91:4-6 "He shall cover thee with his feathers, and under his wings shalt thou trust: his truth shall be thy shield and buckler. Thou shalt not be afraid for the terror by night; nor for the arrow that flieth by day:

Nor for the pestilence that walketh in darkness; nor for the destruction that wasteth at noonday.

Hebrews 13:6 "So that we may boldly say, the Lord is my helper, and I will not fear what man shall do unto me."

Forgiveness

Luke 6:35-38 "But love ye your enemies, and do good, and lend, hoping for nothing again; and your reward shall be great, and ye shall be children of the Highest; for he is kind unto the unthankful and to the evil. Be ye therefore merciful, as your Father also is merciful. Judge not, and ye shall not be judged; condemn not, and ye shall not be condemned; forgive, and ye shall be forgiven."

John 20:23 "Whosesoever sins ye remit, they are remitted unto them; and whosesoever sins ye retain, they are retained."

John 13:10 "Jesus saith to him, He that is washed needeth not save to wash his feet, but is clean every whit; and ye are clean, but not all."

Matthew 6:14 "For if ye forgive men their trespasses, your heavenly Father will also forgive you."

Mark 11:25-26 "And when ye stand praying, forgive, if ye have ought against any: that your Father also which is in heaven may forgive you your trespasses. But if ye do not forgive, neither will your Father which is in heaven forgive your trespasses."

Matthew 5:44-45 "But I say unto you, Love your enemies, bless them that curse you, do good to them that hate you, and pray for them which despitefully use you, and persecute you; That ye may be the children of your Father which is in heaven: for he maketh his sun to rise on the evil and good, and sendeth rain on the just and on the unjust."

Ezekiel 18:22 "All his transgressions that he hath committed, they shall not be mentioned unto him: in his righteousness that he hath done he shall live."

Goodness
Exodus 33:19 "And he said, I will make all my goodness pass before thee, and I will proclaim the name of the Lord before thee; and will be gracious to whom I will be gracious, and will shew mercy on whom I will shew mercy."

Jeremiah 32:41 "Yea, I will rejoice over them to do them good, and I will plant them in this land assuredly with my whole heart and with my whole soul."

<u>Psalm 68:10</u> "…Thou, O God, hast prepared of thy goodness for the poor."

<u>Ephesians 5:9</u> "(For the fruit of the Spirit is in all goodness and righteousness and truth;) Proving what is acceptable unto the Lord."

<u>Romans 2:3-4</u> "And thinkest thou this, O man, that judgest them which do such things, and doest the same, that thou shalt escape the judgment of God? Or despisest thou the riches of his goodness and forbearance and longsuffering; not knowing that the goodness of God leadeth thee to repentance?"

<u>Jeremiah 31:14</u> "And I will satiate the soul of the priests with fatness, and my people shall be satisfied with my goodness, saith the Lord."

<u>2 Thessalonians 1:11</u> "Wherefore also we pray always for you, that our God would count you worthy of this calling, and fulfil all the good pleasure of his goodness, and the work of faith with power:"

<u>Psalm 23:6</u> "Surely goodness and mercy shall follow me all the days of my life: and I will dwell in the house of the Lord forever."

Gossip

<u>Psalm 34:13</u> "Keep thy tongue from evil, and thy lips from speaking guile."

<u>Proverbs 26:20-22</u> "Where no wood is, there the fire goeth out; so where there is no talebearer, the strife ceaseth. As coals are to burning coals, and wood to fire; so is a contentious man to kindle strife. The words of a tale bearer are as wounds, and they go down into the innermost parts of the belly."

<u>Proverbs 11:13</u> "A talebearer revealeth secrets: but he that is of a faithful spirit concealeth the matter."

<u>Psalm 52:2</u> "Thy tongue deviseth mischiefs; like a sharp razor, working deceitfully."

<u>Proverbs 16:28</u> "A froward man soweth strife: and a whisperer separateth chief friends."

<u>Leviticus 19:16</u> "Thou shalt not go up and down as a talebearer among thy people: neither shalt thou stand against the blood of thy neighbor: I am the Lord."

<u>Proverbs 25:23</u> "The north wind driveth away rain: so doth an angry countenance a backbiting tongue."

Proverbs 20:19 "He that goeth about a talebearer revealeth secrets: therefore meddle not with him that flattereth with his lips."

Proverbs 18:21 "Death and life are in the power of the tongue: and they that love it shall eat the fruit thereof."

Proverbs 18:7 "A fool's mouth is his destruction, and his lips are the snare of his soul."

Grace

Romans 3:23-24 "For all have sinned, and come short of the glory of God; Being justified freely by his grace through the redemption that is in Christ Jesus."

Romans 5:20-21 "Moreover the law entered, that the offence might abound. But where sin abounded, grace did much more abound: That as sin hath reigned unto death, even so might grace reign through righteousness unto eternal life by Jesus Christ our Lord."

Romans 6:14 "For sin shall not have dominion over you: for ye are not under the law, but under grace."

2 Corinthians 12:9 "And he said unto me, My grace is sufficient for thee: for my strength is made perfect in weakness. Most gladly therefore will I rather glory in

my infirmities, that the power of Christ may rest upon me."

Ephesians 2:8-9 "For by grace are ye saved through faith; and that not of yourselves: it is the gift of God: Not of works, lest any man should boast."

Titus 3:5-7 "Not by works of righteousness which we have done, but according to his mercy he saved us, by the washing of regeneration, and renewing of the Holy Ghost; Which he shed on us abundantly through Jesus Christ our Savior; That being justified by his grace, we should be made heirs according to the hope of eternal life."

Hebrews 4:16 "Let us therefore come boldly unto the throne of grace, that we may obtain mercy, and find grace to help in time of need."

2 Peter 3:18 "But grow in grace, and in the knowledge of our Lord and Savior Jesus Christ. To him be glory both now and for ever. Amen."

Guidance from God
Proverbs 3:5-6 "Trust in the Lord with all thine heart, and lean not to thine own understanding. In all thy ways acknowledge him, and he shall direct thy paths."

Isaiah 28:26 "For his God doth instruct him to discretion, and doth teach him."

Proverbs 11:5 "The righteousness of the perfect shall direct his way: but the wicked shall fall by his own wickedness."

Proverbs 16:9 "A man's heart deviseth his way: but the Lord directeth his steps."

Psalm 37:23 "The steps of a good man are ordered by the Lord: and he delighteth in his way."

Psalm 48:14 "For this God is our God forever and ever: he will be our guide even unto death."

Isaiah 42:16 "And I will bring the blind by a way that they knew not; I will lead them in the paths that they have not known: I will make darkness light before them, and crooked things straight. These things will I do unto them, and not forsake them."

Isaiah 2:3 "…And he will teach us of his ways, and we will walk in his paths…"

Psalm 32:8 "I will instruct thee and teach thee in the way which thou shalt go: I will guide thee with mine eye."

<u>Psalm 16:7</u> "I will bless the Lord, who hath given me counsel: my reins also instruct me in the night seasons."

Guilt

<u>Exodus 34:6-7</u> "And the Lord passed by before him, and proclaimed, The Lord, The Lord God, merciful and gracious, longsuffering, and abundant in goodness and truth, Keeping mercy for thousands, forgiving iniquity and transgression and sin, and that will by no means clear the guilty; visiting the iniquity of the fathers upon the children, and upon the children's children, unto the third and the forth generation."

<u>Deuteronomy 21:9</u> "So shalt thou put away the guilt of innocent blood from among you, when thou shalt do that which is right in the sight of the Lord."

<u>I Samuel 26:9</u> "And David said to Abishai, Destroy him not: for who can stretch forth his hand against the Lord's anointed, and be guiltless."

<u>Matthew 12:6-7</u> "But I say unto you, That in this place is one greater than the temple. But if ye had known what this meaneth, I will have mercy, and not sacrifice, ye would not have condemned the guiltless."

<u>Romans 8:1</u> "There is therefore now no condemnation to them which are in Christ Jesus, who walk not after the flesh, but after the Spirit."

<u>I John 3:20</u> "For if our heart condemn us, God is greater than our heart, and knoweth all things."

<u>I John 1:9</u> "If we confess our sins, he is faithful and just to forgive us our sins, and to cleanse us from all unrighteousness."

<u>Psalm 103:12</u> "As far as the east is from the west, so far hath he removed our transgressions from us."

Grieving
<u>Lamentations 3:32-33</u> "But though he cause grief, yet will he have compassion according to the multitude of his mercies. For he doth not afflict willingly nor grieve the children of men."

<u>2 Corinthians 1:3-4</u> "Blessed be God, even the Father of our Lord Jesus Christ, the Father of mercies, and the God of all comfort; who comforteth us in all our tribulation, that we may be able to comfort them which are in any trouble, by the comfort wherewith we ourselves are comforted of God."

<u>Psalm 37:39</u> "But the salvation of the righteous is of the Lord: he is their strength in the time of trouble."

<u>Psalm 71:20</u> "Thou, which hast shewed me great and sore troubles, shalt quicken me again, and shalt bring me up again from the depths of the earth."

<u>Psalm 34:19</u> "Many are the afflictions of the righteous, but the Lord delivereth him out of them all."

<u>Psalm 126:5-6</u> "They that sow in tears shall reap in joy. He that goeth forth and weepeth, bearing precious seed, shall doubtless come again with rejoicing, bringing his sheaves with him."

<u>Psalm 22:24</u> "For he hath not despised nor abhorred the affliction of the afflicted; neither hath he hid his face from him; but when he cried unto him, he heard."

Grudges

<u>James 5:9</u> "Grudge not one against another, brethren, lest ye be condemned: behold, the judge standeth before the door."

<u>I Peter 4:8-9</u> "And above all things have fervent charity among yourselves: for charity shall cover the multitude of sins. Use hospitality one to another without grudging."

Psalm 59:15-16 "Let them wander up and down for meat, and grudge if they be not satisfied. But I will sing of thy power: yea, I will sing aloud of thy mercy in the morning: for thou hast been my defence and refuge in the day of my trouble."

Luke 6:37 "Judge not, and ye shall not be judged: condemn not, and ye shall not be condemned: forgive, and ye shall be forgiven."

Romans 12:20 "Therefore if thine enemy hunger, feed him; if he thirst, give him drink…"

Matthew 6:14 "For if ye forgive men their trespasses, your heavenly Father will also forgive you."

Matthew 5:44-45 "But I say unto you, Love your enemies, bless them that curse you, do good to them that hate you, and pray for them which despitefully use you, and persecute you; That ye may be the children of your Father which is in heaven: for he maketh his sun to rise on the evil and on the good, and sendeth rain on the just and on the unjust."

Healing
Isaiah 53:5 "But he was wounded for our transgressions, he was bruised for our iniquities: the

chastisement of our peace was upon him; and with his stripes we are healed."

Jeremiah 17:14 "Heal me, O Lord, and I shall be healed; save me, and I shall be saved: for thou art my praise."

James 5:14-16 "Is any sick among you? let him call for the elders of the church; and let them pray over him, anointing him with oil in the name of the Lord: And the prayer of faith shall save the sick, and the Lord shall raise him up; and if he have committed sins, they shall be forgiven him. Confess your faults one to another, and pray one for another, that ye may be healed. The effectual fervent prayer of a righteous man availeth much."

Matthew 4:23 "And Jesus went about all Galilee, teaching in their synagogues, and preaching the gospel of the kingdom, and healing all manner of sickness and all manner of disease among the people."

Exodus 23:25 "And ye shall serve the Lord your God, and he shall bless thy bread, and thy water; and I will take sickness away from the midst of thee."

<u>Psalm 103:2-3</u> "Bless the Lord, O my soul, and forget not all his benefits: Who forgiveth all thine iniquities; who healeth all thy diseases."

<u>Jeremiah 30:17</u> "For I will restore health unto thee, and I will heal thee of thy wounds, saith the Lord…"

<u>I Corinthians 12:28</u> "And God hath set some in the church, first apostles, secondarily prophets, thirdly teachers, after that miracles, then gifts of healings, helps, governments, diversities of tongues."

<u>I Corinthians 12:8-9</u> "For to one is given by the Spirit the word of wisdom; to another the word of knowledge by the same Spirit; To another faith by the same Spirit; and to another the gifts of healing by the same Spirit."

<u>Holy Spirit</u>
<u>Romans 8:26-27</u> "Likewise the Spirit also helpeth our infirmities: for we know not what we should pray for as we ought: but the Spirit itself maketh intercession for us with groanings which cannot be uttered, And he that searcheth the hearts knoweth what is the mind of the Spirit, because he maketh intercession for the saints according to the will of God."

<u>John 16:13</u> "Howbeit when he, the Spirit of truth, is come, he will guide you into all truth: for he shall not

speak of himself: but whatsoever he shall hear, that shall he speak: and he will show you things to come."

John 14:16-17 "And I will pray the Father, and he shall give you another Comforter, that he may abide with you for ever; Even the Spirit of truth; whom the world cannot receive, because it seeth him not, neither knoweth him: but ye know him; for he dwelleth with you, and shall be in you."

John 7:38-39 "He that believeth on me, as the scripture hath said, out of his belly shall flow rivers of living water. (But this spake he of the Spirit, which they that believe on him should receive: for the Holy Ghost was not yet given; because that Jesus was not yet glorified.)

John 4:14 "But whosoever drinketh of the water that I shall give him shall never thirst: but the water that I shall give him shall be in him a well of water springing up into everlasting life."

Luke 11:13 "If ye then, being evil, know how to give good gifts unto your children: how much more shall your heavenly Father give the Holy Spirit to them that ask him?"

Honesty

<u>Colossians 3:9-10</u> "Lie not one to another, seeing that ye have put off the old man with his deeds; and have put on the new man, which is renewed in knowledge after the image of him that created him."

<u>I Thessalonians 4:6-7</u> "That no man go beyond and defraud his brother in any matter: because that the Lord is the avenger of all such, as we also have forewarned you and testified. For God hath not called us unto uncleanness, but unto holiness."

<u>Proverbs 11:3</u> "The integrity of the upright shall guide them: but the perverseness of transgressors shall destroy them."

<u>Proverbs 11:18</u> "The wicked worketh a deceitful work: but to him that soweth righteousness shall be a sure reward."

<u>Proverbs 12:17</u> "He that speaketh truth sheweth forth righteousness: but a false witness deceit."

<u>Proverbs 12:22</u> "Lying lips are abomination to the Lord; but they that deal truly are his delight."

<u>Leviticus 19:11</u> "Ye shall not steal, neither deal falsely, neither lie one to another."

<u>Leviticus 19:35</u> "Ye shall do no unrighteousness in judgment, in meteyard, in weight, or in measure."

<u>Proverbs 11:1</u> "A false balance is abomination to the Lord: but a just weight is his delight."

<u>Psalm 37:21</u> "The wicked borroweth, and payeth not again: but the righteous sheweth mercy, and giveth."

<u>Hope</u>
<u>Proverbs 13:12</u> "Hope deferred maketh the heart sick: but when the desire cometh, it is a tree of life."

<u>Psalm 31:24</u> "Be of good courage, and he shall strengthen your heart, all ye that hope in the Lord."

<u>Psalm 71:5</u> "For thou art my hope, O Lord God: thou art my trust from my youth."

<u>Psalm 42:11</u> "Why art thou cast down, O my soul? and why art thou disquieted within me? hope thou in God: for I shall yet praise him, who is the health of my countenance, and my God."

<u>I John 3:2-3</u> "Beloved, now are we the sons of God, and it doth not yet appear what we shall be: but we know that, when he shall appear, we shall be like him;

for we shall see him as he is. And every man that hath this hope in him purifieth himself, even as he is pure."

I Peter 1:13 "Wherefore gird up the lions of your mind, be sober, and hope to the end for the grace that is to be brought unto you at the revelation of Jesus Christ;"

Proverbs 14:32 "The wicked is driven away in his wickedness: but the righteous hath hope in his death."

Hebrews 11:1 "Now faith is the substance of things hoped for, the evidence of things not seen."

Romans 4:17-18 "(As it is written, I have made thee a father of many nations,) before him whom he believed, even God, who quickeneth the dead, and calleth those things which be not as though they were. Who against hope believed in hope, that he might become the father of many nations, according to that which was spoken, so shall thy Seed be."

Hospitality
Hebrews 13:2 "Be not forgetful to entertain strangers: for thereby some have entertained angels unawares."

Matthew 25:35-36 "For I was hungred, and ye gave me meat: I was thirsty, and ye gave me drink: I was a stranger, and ye took me in: Naked, and ye clothed me: I was sick, and ye visited me: I was in prison, and ye came unto me."

Mark 9:41 "For whosoever shall give you a cup of water to drink in my name, because ye belong to Christ, verily I say unto you, he shall not lose his reward."

Romans 12:13 "Distributing to the necessity of saints: given to hospitality."

James 2:15-16 "If a brother or sister be naked, and destitute of daily food, And one of you say unto them, Depart in peace, be ye warmed and filled; notwithstanding ye give them not those things which are needful to the body; what doth it profit?"

I John 3:17 "But whoso hath this world's good, and seeth his brother have need, and shutteth up his bowels of compassion from him, how dwelleth the love of God in him?"

Matthew 25:40 "And the King shall answer and say unto them, Verily I say unto you, In as much as ye have done it unto one of the least of these my brethren, ye have done it unto me."

2 Corinthians 8:13-14 "For I mean not that other men be eased, and ye burdened: But by an equality, that now at this time your abundance may be a supply for their want, that their abundance also may be a supply for your want: that there may be equality:"

Humility

I Peter 5:6-7 "Humble yourselves therefore under the mighty hand of God, that he may exalt you in due time: Casting all your care upon him; for he careth for you."

Proverbs 22:4 "By humility and the fear of the Lord are riches, and honor, and life."

Proverbs 16:19 "Better it is to be of a humble spirit with the lowly, than to divide the spoil with the proud."

Proverbs 29:23 "A man's pride shall bring him low: but honour shall uphold the humble in spirit."

Proverbs 15:33 "The fear of the Lord is the instruction of wisdom: and before honor is humility."

Philippians 2:5-8 "Let this mind be in you, which was also in Christ Jesus: Who, being in the form of God, thought it not robbery to be equal with God: But made himself of no reputation, and took upon him the form of a servant, and was made in the likeness of men: And being found in fashion as a man, he humbled himself, and became obedient unto death, even the death of the cross."

Proverbs 3:34 "Surely he scorneth the scorners; but he giveth grace unto the lowly."

Job 22:29-30 "When men are cast down, then thou shalt say, There is lifting up; and he shall save the humble person. He shall deliver the island of the innocent: and it is delivered by the purness of thine hands."

Insanity
2 Timothy 1:7 "For God hath not given us the spirit of fear, but of power, and of love, and of a sound mind."

Isaiah 26:3-4 "Thou wilt keep him in perfect peace, whose mind is stayed on thee: because he trusteth in thee. Trust ye in the Lord forever: for in the Lord Jehovah is everlasting strength:"

Hebrews 12:3 "For consider him that endured such contradiction of sinners against himself, lest ye be wearied and faint in your minds."

<u>Titus 1:15</u> "Unto the pure all things are pure: but unto them that are defiled and unbelieving is nothing pure; but even their mind and conscience is defiled."

<u>Philippians 4:6-7</u> "Be careful for nothing; but in everything by prayer and supplication with thanksgiving let your requests be made known unto God. And the peace of God, which passeth all understanding, shall keep your hearts and minds through Christ Jesus."

<u>I Corinthians 2:16</u> "For who hath known the mind of the Lord, that he may instruct him? But we have the mind of Christ."

<u>Philippians 2:1-3</u> "If there be therefore any consolation in Christ, if any comfort of love, if any fellowship of the Spirit, if any bowels and mercies, Fulfil ye my joy, that ye be likeminded, having the same love, being of one accord, of one mind. Let nothing be done through strife or vainglory; but in lowliness of mind let each esteem other better than themselves."

<u>Joy</u>
<u>Romans 14:17</u> "For the kingdom of God is not meat and drink; but righteousness, and peace and joy in the Holy Ghost."

<u>I Peter 1:8</u> "Whom having not seen, ye love; in whom, though now ye see him not, yet believing, ye rejoice with joy unspeakable and full of glory:"

<u>John 15:11</u> "These things have I spoken unto you, that my joy might remain in you, and that your joy might be full."

<u>Psalm 126:5-6</u> "They that sow in tears shall reap in joy. He that goeth forth and weepeth, bearing precious seed, shall doubtless come again with rejoicing, bringing his sheaves with him."

<u>John 16:22</u> "...I will see you again, and your heart shall rejoice, and your joy no man taketh from you."

<u>Nehemiah 8:10</u> "Then he said unto them, Go your way, eat the fat, and drink the sweet, and send portions unto them for whom nothing is prepared: for this day is holy unto our Lord: neither be ye sorry; for the joy of the Lord is your strength."

<u>Psalm 89:15-16</u> "Blessed is the people that know the joyful sound: they shall walk, O Lord, in the light of thy countenance. In thy name shall they rejoice all the day: in thy righteousness shall they be exalted."

<u>Isaiah 61:10</u> "I will greatly rejoice in the Lord, my soul shall be joyful in my God; for he hath clothed me with garments of salvation, he hath covered me with the robe of righteousness, as a bridegroom decketh himself with ornaments, and as a bride adorneth herself with her jewels."

<u>Jealousy</u>

<u>Proverbs 6:34-35</u> "For jealousy is the rage of a man: therefore he will not spare in the day of vengeance. He will not regard any ransom; neither will he rest content, though thou givest many gifts."

<u>Song of Solomon 8:6</u> "Set me as a seal upon thine heart, as a seal upon thine arm: for love is strong as death; jealousy is cruel as the grave: the coals thereof are coals of fire, which hath a most vehement flame."

<u>Psalm 37:1</u> "Fret not thy self because of evil doers, neither be thou envious against the workers of iniquity."

<u>I Corinthians 13:4-5</u> "Charity suffereth long, and is kind; charity envieth not; charity vaunteth not itself, is not puffed up, Doth not behave itself unseemly, seeketh not her own, is not easily provoked, thinketh no evil;"

<u>Romans 13:13-14</u> "Let us walk honestly, as in the day; not in rioting and drunkenness, not in chambering and wantonness, not in strife and envying. But put ye on the Lord Jesus Christ, and make not provision for the flesh, to fulfil the lusts thereof."

<u>Psalm 79:5</u> "How long, Lord? wilt thou be angry for ever? shall thy jealousy burn like fire?"

Laziness

<u>Proverbs 12:24</u> "The hand of the diligent shall bear rule: but the slothful shall be under tribute."

<u>Proverbs 12:11</u> "He that tilleth his land shall be satisfied with bread: but he that followeth vain persons is void of understanding."

<u>Proverbs 13:4</u> "The soul of the sluggard desireth, and hath nothing: but the soul of the diligent shall be made fat."

<u>Proverbs 15:19</u> "The way of the slothful man is as an hedge of thorns: but the way of the righteous is made plain."

<u>Proverbs 20:13</u> "Love not sleep, lest thou come to poverty; open thine eyes, and thou shalt be satisfied with bread."

<u>Proverbs 10:4-5</u> "He becometh poor that dealeth with a slack hand: but the hand of the diligent maketh rich. He that gathereth in summer is a wise son: but he that sleepeth in harvest is a son that causeth shame."

<u>Proverbs 27:23</u> "Be thou diligent to know the state of thy flocks, and look well to thy herds."

<u>Proverbs 21:5</u> "The thoughts of the diligent tend only to plenteousness; but of everyone that is hasty only to want."

<u>Ephesians 4:28</u> "Let him that stole steal no more: but rather let him labour, working with his hands the thing which is good, that he may have to give to him that needeth."

<u>Romans 12:11</u> "Not slothful in business; fervent in spirit; serving the Lord;"

<u>Proverbs 28:19</u> "He that tilleth his land shall have plenty of bread; but he that followeth after vain persons shall have poverty enough."

Loneliness
<u>John 14:16-17</u> "And I will pray the Father, and he shall give you another Comforter, that he may abide with you forever; Even the Spirit of truth; whom the

world cannot receive, because it seeth him not, neither knoweth him; but ye know him; for he dwelleth with you, and shall be in you."

Isaiah 58:9 "Then shalt thou call, and the Lord shall answer; thou shalt cry, and he shall say, Here I am..."

John 14:18 "I will not leave you comfortless: I will come to you."

Jeremiah 29:12-14 "Then shall ye call upon me, and ye shall go and pray unto me, and I will hearken unto you. And ye shall seek me, and find me, when ye shall search for me with all your heart. And I will be found of you, saith the Lord: and I will turn away your captivity, and I will gather you from all the nations, and from all the places whither I have driven you, saith the Lord; and I will bring you again into the place whence I caused you to be carried away captive."

2 Corinthians 6:18 "And will be a Father unto you, and ye shall be my sons and daughters, saith the Lord Almighty."

2 Corinthians 6:16 "And what agreement hath the temple of God with idols? For ye are the temple of the living God; as God hath said, I will dwell in them, and

walk in them; and I will be their God, and they shall be my people."

Colossians 2:10 "And ye are complete in him, which is the head of all principality and power:"

Long Life
Deuteronomy 5:33 "Ye shall walk in all the ways which the Lord your God hath commanded you, that ye may live, and that it may be well with you, and that ye may prolong your days in the land which ye shall possess."

Psalm 91:16 "With long life will I satisfy him, and show him my salvation."

Proverbs 3:1-2 "My Son, forget not my law; but let thine heart keep my commandments: For length of days, and long life, and peace, shall they add to thee."

Proverbs 9:11 "For by me thy days shall be multiplied, and the years of thy life shall be increased."

Proverbs 10:27 "The fear of the Lord prolongeth days: but the years of the wicked shall be shortened."

Proverbs 17:6 "Children's children are the crown of old men; and the glory of children are their fathers."

<u>Proverbs 20:29</u> "The glory of young men is their strength: and the beauty of old men is the grey head."

<u>Job 11:17</u> "And thine age shall be clearer than the noonday; thou shalt shine forth, thou shalt be as the morning."

<u>Psalm 71:17-18</u> "O God, thou hast taught me from my youth: and hitherto have I declared thy wonderous works. Now also when I am old and greyheaded, O God, forsake me not; until I have shewed thy strength unto this generation, and thy power to everyone that is to come."

<u>Job 5:26</u> "Thou shalt come to thy grave in a full age, like as a shock of corn cometh in his season."

<u>Love</u>
<u>I John 4:18</u> "There is no fear in Love; but perfect love casteth out fear;…"

<u>I John 4:7-10</u> "Beloved, let us love one another: for love is of God; and everyone that loveth is born of God, and knoweth God. He that loveth not knoweth not God; for God is love. In this was manifested the love of God toward us, because that God sent his only begotten Son into the world, that we might live through him. Herein is love, not that we loved God,

but that he loved us, and sent his Son to be the propitiation for our sins."

Deuteronomy 6:5 "And thou shalt love the Lord thy God with all thine heart, and with all thy soul, and with all thy might."

Ephesians 5:2 "And walk in love, as Christ also hath loved us, and hath given himself for us an offering and a sacrifice to God for a sweet smelling savour."

I Corinthians 13:13 "And now abideth faith, hope, charity, these three; but the greatest of these is charity."

I Corinthians 13:3-8 "And though I bestow all my goods to feed the poor, and though I give my body to be burned, and have not charity, it profiteth me nothing. Charity suffereth long, and is kind; charity envieth not; charity vaunteth not itself, is not puffed up, Doth not behave itself unseemly, seeketh not her own, is not easily provoked, thinketh no evil; Rejoiceth not in iniquity, but rejoiceth in the truth; Beareth all things, believeth all things, hopeth all things, endureth all things. Charity never faileth: but whether there be prophecies, they shall fail; whether there be tounges, they shall cease; whether there be knowledge, it shall vanish away."

<u>Proverbs 17:17</u> "A friend loveth at all times, and a brother is born for adversity."

<u>John 13:34</u> "A new commandment I give unto you, that ye love one another; as I have loved you, that ye also love one another. By this shall all men know that ye are my disciples, if ye have love one to another."

<u>Lust</u>

<u>Matthew 5:27-28</u> "Ye have heard that it was said by them of old time, Thou shalt not commit adultery: But I say unto you, that whosoever looketh on a woman to lust after her hath committed adultery with her already in his heart."

<u>Galatians 5:16-17</u> "This I say then, Walk in the Spirit, and ye shall not fulfil the lust of the flesh. For the flesh lusteth against the Spirit, and the Spirit against the flesh: and these are contrary the one to the other: so that ye cannot do the things that ye would."

<u>Galatians 5:24</u> "And they that are Christ's have crucified the flesh with the affections and lusts."

<u>2 Timothy 2:22</u> "Flee also youthful lusts: but follow righteousness, faith, charity, peace, with them that call on the Lord out of a pure heart."

<u>James 1:13-15</u> "Let no man say when he is tempted, I am tempted of God: for God cannot be tempted with evil, neither tempteth he any man: But every man is tempted, when he is drawn away of his own lusts, and enticed. Then when lust have conceived, it bringeth forth sin: and sin, when it is finished, bringeth forth death."

<u>I John 2:16-17</u> "For all that is in the world, the lust of the flesh, and the lust of the eyes, and the pride of life, is not of the Father, but is of the world. And the world passeth away, and the lust thereof; but he that doeth the will of God abideth forever."

<u>I Peter 2:11</u> "Dearly beloved, I beseech you as strangers and pilgrims, abstain from fleshly lust, which war against the soul."

<u>I Corinthians 10:6</u> "Now these things were our examples, to the intent we should not lust after evil things, as they also lusted."

Marriage
<u>Genesis 2:24</u> "Therefore shall a man leave his father and his mother, and shall cleave unto his wife: and they shall be one flesh."

<u>Proverbs 5:18-19</u> "Let thy fountain be blessed: and rejoice with the wife of thy youth. Let her be as the loving hind and pleasant roe; let her breasts satisfy thee at all times; and be thou ravished always with her love."

<u>I Peter 3:1</u> "Likewise, ye wives, be in subjection to your own husbands; that, if any obey not the word, they also may without the word be won by the conversation of the wives;"

<u>I Peter 3:7</u> "Likewise, ye husbands, dwell with them according to knowledge, giving honour unto the wife, as unto the weaker vessel, and as being heirs together of the grace of life; that your prayers be not hindered."

<u>Hebrews 13:4</u> "Marriage is honorable in all, and the bed undefiled; but whoremongers and adulterers God will judge."

<u>Colossians 3:18-19</u> "Wives, submit yourselves unto your own husbands, as it is fit in the Lord. Husbands, love your wives, and be not bitter against them."

<u>Ephesians 5:22-25</u> "Wives, submit yourselves unto your own husband; as unto the Lord. For the husband is the head of the wife, even as Christ is the head of the church: and he is the saviour of the body. Therefore as

the church is subject unto Christ, so let the wives be to their own husbands in everything. Husbands, love your wives, even as Christ also loved the church, and gave himself for it;"

Meekness

I Timothy 6:11 "But thou, O man of God, flee these things; and follow after righteousness, godliness, faith, love, patience, meekness."

II Timothy 2:24-25 "And the servant of the Lord must not strive; but be gentle unto all men, apt to teach, patient, In meekness instructing those that oppose themselves; if God peradventure will give them repentance to the acknowledging of the truth;"

Titus 3:1-2 "Put them in mind to be subject to principalities and powers, to obey magistrates, to be ready to every good work, To speak evil of no man, to be no brawlers, but gentle, showing all meekness unto all men."

James 1:21 "Wherefore lay apart all filthiness and superfluity of naughtiness, and receive with meekness the engrafted word, which is able to save your souls."

<u>James 3:13</u> "Who is a wise man and endued with knowledge among you? let him shew out of a good conversation his works with meekness of wisdom."

<u>Colossians 3:12-13</u> "Put on therefore, as the elect of God, holy and beloved, bowels of mercies, kindness, humbleness of mind, meekness, longsuffering; Forbearing one another, and forgiving one another, if any man have a quarrel against any: even as Christ forgave you, so also do ye."

<u>Galatians 5:22-23</u> "But the fruit of the Spirit is love, joy, peace, longsuffering, gentleness, goodness, faith, meekness, temperance: against such there is no law."

<u>Mercy</u>
<u>Exodus 34:6-7</u> "And the Lord passed by before him, and proclaimed, The Lord, The Lord God, merciful and gracious, longsuffering, and abundant in goodness and truth, keeping mercy for thousands, forgiving iniquity and transgression and sin, and that will by no means clear the guilty; visiting the iniquity of the fathers upon the children, and upon the children's children, unto the third and to the fourth generation."

<u>Psalm 23:6</u> "Surely goodness and mercy shall follow me all the days of my life: and I will dwell in the house of the Lord forever."

<u>Proverbs 20:28</u> "Mercy and truth preserve the King and his throne is upholden by mercy."

<u>Luke 1:49-50</u> "For he that is mighty hath done to me great things; and holy is his name. And his mercy is on them that fear him from generation to generation."

<u>Isaiah 60:10</u> "...For in my wrath I smote thee, but in my favour have I had mercy on thee."

<u>Psalm 103:17</u> "But the mercy of the Lord is from everlasting to everlasting upon them that fear him, and his righteousness unto children's children."

<u>Hosea 2:23</u> "...And I will have mercy upon her that had not obtained mercy; and I will say to them which were not my people, Thou art my people; and they shall say, Thou art my God.

<u>Isaiah 48:9</u> "For my name's sake will I defer mine anger, and for my praise will I refrain for thee, that I cut thee not off."

Money
<u>Ecclesiastes 10:19</u> "A feast is made for laughter, and wine maketh merry: but money answereth all things."

<u>Proverbs 15:16</u> "Better is little with fear of the Lord then great treasure and trouble therewith."

<u>I Timothy 6:10-11</u> "For the love of money is the root of all evil: which while some coveted after, they have erred from the faith, and pierced themselves through with many sorrows. But thou, O man of God, flee these things; and follow after righteousness, godliness, faith, love, patience, meekness."

<u>Proverbs 23:4-5</u> "Labour not to be rich: cease from thine own wisdom. Wilt thou set thine eyes upon that which is not? For riches certainly make themselves wings; they fly away as an eagle toward heaven."

<u>I Timothy 6:17-19</u> "Charge them that are rich in this world, that they be not highminded, nor trust in uncertain riches, but in the living God, who giveth us richly all things to enjoy; That they do good, that they be rich in good works, ready to distribute, willing to communicate; Laying up in store for themselves a good foundation against the time to come, that they may lay hold on eternal life."

<u>Proverbs 22:2</u> "The rich and poor meet together: the Lord is the maker of them all."

<u>Ecclesiastes 5:19</u> "Every man also to whom God hath given riches and wealth, and hath given him power to eat thereof, and to take his portion, and to rejoice in his labour; this is the gift of God."

<u>Ecclesiastes 5:13</u> "There is a sore evil which I have seen under the sun, namely, riches kept for the owners thereof to their hurt."

<u>Mourning</u>

<u>Psalm 30:11</u> "Thou hast turned for me my mourning into dancing: thou hast put off my sack cloth, and girded me with gladness;"

<u>Isaiah 61:1-3</u> "The spirit of the Lord God is upon me; because the Lord hath anointed me to preach good tidings unto the meek; he hath sent me to bind up the brokenhearted, to proclaim liberty to the captives, and the opening of the prison to them that are bound; To proclaim the acceptable year of the Lord, and the day of vengeance of our God; to comfort all that mourn; To appoint unto them that mourn in Zion, to give unto them beauty for ashes, the oil of joy for mourning, the garment of praise for the spirit of heaviness; that they might be called trees of righteousness, the planting of the Lord, that he might be glorified."

Jeremiah 31:13-14 "Then shall the virgin rejoice in the dance, both young men and old together: for I will turn their mourning into joy, and will comfort them, and make them rejoice from their sorrow. And I will satiate the soul of the priests with fatness, and my people shall be satisfied with my goodness, saith the Lord."

James 4:9-10 "Be afflicted, and mourn, and weep: let your laughter be turned to mourning, and your joy to heaviness. Humble yourselves in the sight of the Lord, and he shall lift you up."

Matthew 5:4 "Blessed are they that mourn: for they shall be comforted."

Isaiah 57:18-19 "I have seen his ways, and will heal him: I will lead him also, and restore comforts unto him and to his mourners. I create the fruit of the lips; Peace, peace to him that is far off, and to him that is near, saith the Lord; and I will heal him."

Obedience
Acts 5:29 "Then Peter and the other apostles answered and said, We ought to obey God rather than men."

Romans 5:19 "For as by one man's disobedience many were made sinners, so by the obedience of one shall many be made righteous."

Romans 6:16-17 "Know ye not, that to whom ye yield yourselves servants to obey, his servants ye are to whom ye obey; whether of sin unto death, or of obedience unto righteousness? But God be thanked, that ye were the servants of sin, but ye have obeyed from the heart that form of doctrine which was delivered you."

Ephesians 6:1 "Children, obey your parents in the Lord: for this is right."

Ephesians 6:5 "Servants, be obedient to them that are your masters according to the flesh, with fear and trembling, in singleness of your heart, as unto Christ;"

Isaiah 1:19 "If ye be willing and obedient, ye shall eat the good of the land:"

I Samuel 15:22 "And Samuel said, Hath the Lord as great delight in burnt offerings and sacrifices, as in obeying the voice of the Lord? Behold, to obey is better than sacrifice, and to hearken than the fat of rams."

Job 36:11 "If they obey and serve him, they shall spend their days in prosperity, and their years in pleasures."

Deuteronomy 29:9 "Keep therefore the words of this covenant, and do them, that ye may prosper in all that ye do."

Oppression

Exodus 22:21-22 "Thou shalt neither vex a stranger, nor oppress him: for ye were strangers in the hand of Egypt. Ye shall not afflict any widow, or the fatherless child."

Leviticus 25:14 "And if thou sell ought unto thy neighbour, or buyest ought of thy neighbour's hand, ye shall not oppress one another."

Deuteronomy 26:7 "And when we cried unto the Lord God of our fathers, the Lord heard our voice, and looked on our affliction, and our labour, and our oppression:"

Psalm 9:9 "The Lord also will be a refuge for the oppressed, a refuge in times of trouble."

Psalm 10:17-18 "Lord, thou hast heard the desire of the humble: thou wilt prepare their heart, thou wilt cause thine ear to hear: To judge the fatherless and the oppressed, that the man of the earth may no more oppress."

Ecclesiastes 7:7 "Surely oppression maketh a wise man mad; and a gift destroyeth the heart."

Acts 10:38 "How God anointed Jesus of Nazareth with the Holy Ghost and with power: who went about doing good, and healing all that were oppressed of the devil; for God was with him."

Psalm 146:8 "The Lord openeth the eyes of the blind; the Lord raiseth them that are bowed down: the Lord loveth the righteous;"

Psalm 73:26 "My flesh and my heart faileth: but God is the strength of my heart, and my portion forever."

Patience

Romans 5:3-5 "And not only so, but we glory in tribulations also: knowing that tribulation worketh patience; And patience, experience; and experience, hope: And hope maketh not ashamed; because the love of God is shed abroad in our hearts by the Holy Ghost which is given unto us."

Romans 8:25 "But if we hope for that we see not, then do we with patience wait for it."

Romans 15:4-5 "For whatsoever things were written aforetime were written for our learning, that we through patience and comfort of the scriptures might have hope. Now the God of patience and consolation grant you to be like minded one toward another according to Christ Jesus:"

I Thessalonians 5:14 "Now we exhort you, brethren, warn them that are unruly, comfort the feebleminded, support the weak, be patient toward all men."

I Timothy 6:11 "But thou, O man of God, flee these things; and follow after righteousness, godliness, faith, love, patience, meekness."

Hebrews 6:11-12 "And we desire that everyone of you do shew the same diligence to the full assurance of hope unto the end; That ye be not slothful, but followers of them who through faith and patience inherit the promises."

Hebrews 10:36 "For ye have need of patience, that, after ye have done the will of God, ye might receive the promise."

Galatians 6:9 "And let us not be weary in well doing: for in due season we shall reap, if we faint not."

Peace

Peace

<u>2 Thessalonians 3:16</u> "Now the Lord of peace himself give you peace always by all means…"

<u>Colossians 3:15</u> "And let the peace of God rule in your hearts, to the which also ye are called in one body; and be ye thankful."

<u>Psalm 34:14</u> "Depart from evil, and do good; seek peace, and pursue it."

<u>John 14:27</u> "Peace I leave with you, my peace I give unto you: not as the world giveth, give I unto you. Let not your heart be troubled, neither let it be afraid."

<u>Proverbs 16:7</u> "When a man's ways please the Lord, he maketh even his enemies to be at peace with him.

<u>Philippians 4:7</u> "And the peace of God, which passeth all understanding, shall keep your hearts and minds through Christ Jesus."

<u>Psalms 85:8</u> "I will hear what God the Lord will speak: for he will speak peace unto his people, and to his saints:"

Galatians 5:22-23 "But the fruit of the Spirit is love, joy, peace, longsuffering, gentleness, goodness, faith, meekness, temperance: against such there is no law."

Psalm 37:37 "Mark the perfect man, and behold the upright: for the end of that man is peace."

Mark 9:50 "Salt is good: but if the salt have lost his saltness, wherewith will ye season it? Have salt in yourselves, and have peace one with another."

Prayer
Matthew 6:6 "But thou, when thou prayest, enter into thy closet, and when thou hast shut thy door, pray to thy Father which is in secret; and thy Father which seeth in secret shall reward thee openly."

Psalm 55:17 "Evening, and morning, and at noon, will I pray, and cry aloud: and he shall hear my voice."

John 15:7 "If ye abide in me, and my words abide in you, ye shall ask what ye will, and it shall be done unto you."

James 5:16 "Confess your faults one to another, and pray one for another, that ye may be healed. The effectual fervent prayer of a righteous man availeth much."

Matthew 21:22 "And all things, whatsoever ye shall ask in prayer, believing, ye shall receive."

Psalm 145:18-19 "The Lord is nigh unto all them that call upon him, to all that call upon him in truth. He will fulfil the desire of them that fear him: he also will hear their cry, and will save them."

John 14:13-14 "And whatsoever ye shall ask in my name, that will I do, that the Father may be glorified in the Son. If ye shall ask anything in my name, I will do it."

Jeremiah 29:12 "Then shall ye call upon me, and ye shall go and pray unto me, and I will hearken unto you."

2 Chronicles 7:14 "If my people, which are called by name, shall humble themselves, and pray, and seek my face, and turn from their wicked ways; then I will hear from heaven, and will forgive their sin, and will heal their land."

Pride
Proverbs 8:13 "The fear of the Lord is to hate evil: pride, and arrogancy, and the evil way, and the forward mouth, do I hate."

<u>Luke 16:15</u> "And he said unto them, Ye are they which justify yourselves before men; but God knoweth your hearts: for that which is highly esteemed among men is abomination in the sight of God."

<u>Proverbs 11:2</u> "When pride cometh, then cometh shame: but with the lowly is wisdom."

<u>2 Corinthians 10:17-18</u> "But he that glorieth, let him glory in the Lord. For not he that commendeth himself approved, but whom the Lord commendeth."

<u>Proverbs 13:10</u> "Only by pride cometh contention: but with the well advised is wisdom."

<u>John 5:44</u> "How can ye believe, which receive honor one of another, and seek not the honor that cometh from God only?

<u>Proverbs 16:18</u> "Pride goeth before destruction, and an haughty spirit before a fall."

<u>Mark 9:35</u> "And he sat down; and called the twelve, and saith unto them, If any man desire to be first, the same shall be last of all, and servant of all."

<u>Proverbs 29:23</u> "A man's pride shall bring him low: but honour shall uphold the humble in spirit."

I John 2:16 "For all that is in the world, the lust of the flesh, and the lust of the eyes, and the pride of life, is not of the Father, but is of the world."

Protection

Isaiah 54:17 "No weapon that is formed against thee shall prosper; and every tongue that shall rise against thee in judgment thou shalt condemn. This is the heritage of the servants of the Lord, and their righteousness is of me, saith the Lord."

Deuteronomy 20:4 "For the Lord your God is he that goeth with you, to fight for you against your enemies, to save you."

Deuteronomy 28:7 "The Lord shall cause thine enemies that rise up against thee to be smitten before thy face: they shall come out against thee one way, and flee before thee seven ways."

Joshua 1:5 "There shall not any man be able to stand before thee all the days of thy life: as I was with Moses, so I will be with thee: I will not fail thee, nor forsake thee."

Psalm 91:9-10 "Because thou hast made the Lord, which is my refuge, even the most High, thy habitation; There shall no evil befall thee, neither shall any plague come nigh thy dwelling."

Job 22:25 "Yea, the Almighty shall be thy defense, and thou shalt have plenty of silver."

Psalm 18:2 "The Lord is my rock, and my fortress, and my deliver; my God, my strength, in whom I will trust; my buckler, and the horn of my salvation, and my high tower."

Psalm 4:8 "I will both lay me down in peace, and sleep: for thou, Lord, only makest me dwell in safety."

Psalm 112:7 "He shall be not be afraid of evil tidings: his heart is fixed, trusting in the Lord."

Proverbs 3:24 "When thou liest down, thou shalt not be afraid: yea, thou shalt lie down, and thy sleep shall be sweet."

Repentance
Matthew 9:13 "But go ye and learn what that meaneth, I will have mercy, and not sacrifice; for I am not come to call the righteous, but sinners to repentance."

Luke 24:46-47 "And said unto them, Thus it is written, and thus it behoved Christ to suffer, and to rise from the dead on the third day: And that repentance and remission of sins should be preached in his name among all nations, beginning at Jerusalem."

<u>Romans 2:3-4</u> "And thinkest thou this, O man, that judgest them which do such things, and doest the same, that thou shalt escape the judgment of God? Or despisest thou the riches of his goodness and forbearance and longsuffering; not knowing that the goodness of God leadeth thee to repentance?"

<u>2 Corinthians 7:10</u> "For godly sorrow worketh repentance to salvation not to be repented of: but the sorrow of the world worketh death."

<u>2 Peter 3:9</u> "The Lord is not slack concerning his promise, as some men count slackness; but is longsuffering to us-ward, not willing that any should perish, but that all should come to repentance."

<u>Mark 1:15</u> "…The time is fulfilled, and the kingdom of God is at hand: repent ye, and believe the gospel."

<u>Ezekiel 18:21-22</u> "But if the wicked will turn from all his sins that he hath committed, and keep all my statutes, and do that which is lawful and right, he shall surely live, he shall not die. All his transgressions that he hath

committed, they shall not be mentioned unto him: in his righteousness that he hath done he shall live."

Mark 6:12 "And they went out, and preached that men should repent."

Resurrection

Revelation 20:4-5 "And I saw thrones, and they sat upon them, and judgment was given unto them: and I saw the souls of them that were beheaded for the witness of Jesus, and for the word of God, and which had not worshipped the beast, neither his image, neither had received his mark upon their foreheads, or in their hands; and they lived and reigned with Christ a thousand years. But the rest of the dead lived not again until the thousand years were finished. This is the first resurrection."

2 Timothy 2:8-10 "Remember that Jesus Christ of the seed of David was raised from the dead according to my gospel: Wherein I suffer trouble, as an evil doer, even unto bonds; but the word of God is not bound. Therefore I endure all things for the elect's sakes, that they may also obtain the salvation which is in Christ Jesus with eternal glory."

Philippians 3:10-11 "That I may know him, and the power of his resurrection, and the fellowship of his sufferings, being made conformable unto his death; If by any means I might attain unto the resurrection of the dead."

Luke 20:35-36 "But they which shall be accounted worthy to obtain that world, and the resurrection from the dead, neither marry, nor are given in marriage: Neither can they die any more: for they are equal unto the angels; and are the children of God, being the children of resurrection."

Luke 24:5-7 "And as they were afraid, and bowed down their faces to the earth, they said unto them, Why seek ye the living among the dead? He is not here, but is risen: remember how he spake unto you when he was yet in Galilee, Saying, The Son of man must be delivered into the hands of sinful men, and be crucified, and the third day rise again."

Righteousness

Matthew 6:33 "But seek ye first the kingdom of God, and his righteousness; And all these things shall be added unto you."

Romans 1:17 "For therein is the righteousness of God revealed from faith to faith: as it is written, The just shall live by faith."

<u>Proverbs 10:24</u> "The fear of the wicked, it shall come upon him: but the desire of the righteous shall be granted."

<u>Romans 6:12-13</u> "Let not sin therefore reign in your mortal body, that ye should obey it in the lust thereof. Neither yield ye your members as instruments of unrighteousness unto sin: but yield yourselves unto God, as those that are alive from the dead, and your members as instruments of righteousness unto God."

<u>Psalm 5:12</u> "For thou, Lord, wilt bless the righteous; with favour wilt thou compass him as with a shield."

<u>Romans 10:3-4</u> "For they being ignorant of God's righteousness, and going about to establish their own righteousness have not submitted themselves unto the righteousness of God. For Christ is the end of the law for righteousness to everyone that believeth."

<u>Romans 14:17</u> "For the kingdom of God is not meat and drink; but righteousness, and peace, and joy in the Holy Ghost."

<u>Galatians 2:16</u> "Knowing that a man is not justified by the works of the law, but by the faith of Jesus Christ, even we have believed in Jesus Christ, that we might be justified by the faith of Christ, and not by the works

of the law: for by the works of the law shall no flesh be justified."

<u>Romans 8:32</u> "He that spared not his own Son, but delivered him up for us all, how shall he not with him also freely give us all things?

<u>Salvation</u>
<u>I Timothy 2:3-4</u> "For this is good and acceptable in the sight of God our Saviour; who will have all men to be saved, and to come unto the knowledge of the truth."

<u>John 3:16</u> "For God so loved the world, that he gave his only begotten Son, that whosoever believeth on him shall not perish, but have everlasting life."

<u>John 1:12-13</u> "But as many as received him, to them gave he power to become the sons of God, even to them that believe on his name: which were born, not of blood, nor of the will of the flesh, nor of the will of man, but of God."

<u>Romans 10:9</u> "That if thou shalt confess with thy mouth the Lord Jesus, and shalt believe in thine heart that God hath raised him from the dead, thou shalt be saved."

<u>Romans 10:13</u> "For whosoever shall call upon the name of the Lord shall be saved."

<u>Romans 1:16</u> "For I am not ashamed of the gospel of Christ: for it is the power of God unto salvation to everyone that believeth; to the Jew first, and also to the Greek."

<u>John 3:3-6</u> "Jesus answered and said unto him, Verily, verily, I say unto thee, Except a man be born again, he cannot see the kingdom of God. Nicodemus saith unto him, How can a man be born when he is old? Can he enter the second time into his mother's womb, and be born? Jesus answered, Verily, verily, I say unto thee, Except a man be born of water and of the Spirit, he cannot enter into the kingdom of God. That which is born of the flesh is flesh; and that which is born of the Spirit is spirit."

<u>Seeking God</u>
<u>Luke 11:9-10</u> "And I say unto you, Ask, and it shall be given you; seek, and ye shall find; knock, and it shall be opened unto you. For everyone that asketh receiveth; and he that seeketh findeth; and to him that knocketh it shall be opened."

<u>Hebrews 11:6</u> "But without faith it is impossible to please him: for he that cometh to God must believe

that he is, and that he is a rewarder of them that diligently seek him."

John 15:4-5 "Abide in me, and I in you. As the branch cannot bear fruit of itself, except it abide in the vine; no more can ye, except ye abide in me. I am the vine, ye are the branches: He that abideth in me, and I in him, the same bringeth forth much fruit: for without me ye can do nothing."

Psalm 9:10 "And they that know thy name will put their trust in thee: for thou, Lord, hast not forsaken them that seek thee."

Jeremiah 29:12-13 "Then shall ye call upon me, and ye shall go and pray unto me, and I will hearken unto you. And ye shall seek me, and find me, when ye shall search for me with all your heart."

Lamentations 3:25 "The Lord is good unto them that wait for him, to the soul that seeketh him."

Acts 17:27 "That they should seek the Lord, if haply they might feel after him, and find him, though he be not far from every one of us:"

Matthew 5:6 "Blessed are they which do hunger and thirst after righteousness: for they shall be filled."

Sexual Sins

I Corinthians 6:15-16 "Know ye not that your bodies are the members of Christ? Shall I then take members of Christ, and make them members of an harlot? God forbid. What? Know ye not that he which is joined to an harlot is one body? For two, saith he, shall be one flesh."

I Thessalonians 4:3 "For this is the will of God, even your sanctification, that ye should abstain from fornication:"

I Corinthians 6:9-10 "Know ye not that the unrighteous shall not inherit the kingdom of God? Be not deceived: neither fornicators, nor idolaters, nor adulterers, nor effeminate, nor abusers of themselves with mankind, nor thieves, nor covetous, nor drunkards, nor revilers, nor extortioners, shall inherit the kingdom of God."

James 1:12 "Blessed is the man that endureth temptation: for when he is tried, he shall receive the crown of life, which the Lord hath promised to them that love him."

I Corinthians 6:18 "Flee fornication. Every sin that a man doeth is without the body; but he that committeth fornication sinneth against his own body."

II Corinthians 6:14 "Be ye not unequally yoked together with unbelievers: for what fellowship hath righteousness with unrighteousness? and what communion hath light with darkness?"

2 Timothy 2:22 "Flee also youthful lust: but follow righteousness, faith, charity, peace, with them that call on the Lord out of a pure heart."

Shame

Mark 8:38 "Whosoever therefore shall be ashamed of me and of my words in this adulterous and sinful generation; of him also shall the Son of man be ashamed, when he cometh in the glory of his Father with the holy angels."

Psalm 119:80 "Let my heart be sound in thy statutes; that I be not ashamed."

Romans 1:16 "For I am not ashamed of the gospel of Christ; for it is the power of God unto salvation to everyone that believeth; to the Jew first, and also to the Greek."

I Peter 4:16 "Yet if any man suffer as a Christian, let him not be ashamed; but let him glorify God on this behalf."

<u>Romans 5:5</u> "And hope maketh not ashamed; because the love of God is shed abroad in our hearts by the Holy Ghost which is given unto us."

<u>Hebrews 4:16</u> "Let us therefore come boldly unto the throne of grace, that we may obtain mercy, and find grace to help in time of need."

<u>Romans 9:33</u> "As it is written, Behold, I lay in Sion a stumbling stone and rock of offense: and whosoever believeth on him shall not be ashamed."

<u>Psalm 119:6</u> "Then shall I not be ashamed, when I have respect unto all thy commandments."

<u>2 Timothy 2:15</u> "Study to show thyself approved unto God, a workman that needeth not to be ashamed, rightly dividing the word of truth."

<u>Sin</u>

<u>Romans 6:6-7</u> "Knowing this, that our old man is crucified with him, that the body of sin might be destroyed, that henceforth we should not serve sin. For he that is dead is freed from sin."

<u>I Timothy 1:15</u> "This is a faithful saying, and worthy of all acceptation, that Christ Jesus came into the world to save sinners; of whom I am chief."

<u>Ephesians 1:7</u> "In whom we have redemption through his blood, the forgiveness of sins, according to the riches of his grace;"

<u>Romans 6:14</u> "For sin shall not have dominion over you: for ye are not under the law, but under grace."

<u>I John 2:1-2</u> "...And if any man sin, we have an advocate with the Father, Jesus Christ the righteous: And he is the propitiation for our sins: and not for ours only, but also for the sins of the whole world."

<u>Romans 6:1-2</u> "What shall we say then? Shall we continue in sin, that grace may abound? God forbid. How shall we, that are dead to sin, live any longer therein?"

<u>I John 3:5</u> "And ye know that he was manifested to take away our sins; and in him is no sin."

<u>2 Corinthians 5:17</u> "Therefore if any man be in Christ, he is a new creature: old things are passed away; behold, all things are become new."

<u>Matthew 1:21</u> "And she shall bring forth a son, and thou shalt call his name Jesus: for he shall save his people from their sins."

Success

Malachi 3:10 "Bring ye all the tithes into the storehouse, that there may be meat in my house, and prove me now herewith, saith the Lord of hosts, if I will not open you the windows of heaven, and pour you out a blessing, that there shall not be room enough to receive it."

Psalm 112:3 "Wealth and riches shall be in his house: and his righteousness endureth forever."

Joshua 1:8 "This book of the law shall not depart out of thy mouth; but thou shalt meditate therein day and night, that thou mayest observe to do according to all that is written therein: for then thou shalt make thy way prosperous, and then thou shalt have good success."

Deuteronomy 28:8 "The Lord shall command the blessing upon thee in thy storehouses, and in all that thou settest thine hand unto; and he shall bless thee in the land which the Lord thy God giveth thee."

Proverbs 22:4 "By humility and the fear of the Lord are riches, and honour, and life."

Deuteronomy 28:11-12 "And the Lord shall make thee plenteous in goods, in the fruit of thy body, and in the fruit of thy cattle, and in the fruit of thy ground, in the land which the Lord sware unto thy fathers to give thee. The Lord shall open unto thee his good treasure, the heaven to give the rain unto thy land in his season, and to bless all the works of thine hand: and thou shalt lend unto many nations, and thou shalt not borrow."

Deuteronomy 8:18 "But thou shalt remember the Lord thy God: for it is he that giveth thee power to get wealth, that he may establish his covenant which he sware unto thy fathers, as it is this day."

Temptation
Revelation 3:10 "Because thou hast kept the word of my patience, I will also keep thee from the hour of temptation, which shall come upon all the world, to try them that dwell upon the earth."

I Peter 1:6-7 "Wherein ye greatly rejoice, though now for a season, if need be, ye are in heaviness through manifold temptations: That the trial of your faith, being much more precious than of gold that perisheth, though it be tried with fire, might be found unto praise and honour, and glory at the appearing of Jesus Christ."

<u>James 1:2-3</u> "My brethren, count it all joy when ye fall into divers temptations; Knowing this, that the trying of your faith worketh patience."

<u>James 1:12</u> "Blessed is the man that endureth temptation: for when he is tried, he shall receive the crown of life, which the Lord hath promised to them that love him."

<u>Hebrews 3:8</u> "Harden not your hearts, as in the provocation, in the day of temptation in the wilderness;"

<u>James 1:13-14</u> "Let no man say when he is tempted, I am tempted of God: for God cannot be tempted with evil, neither tempteth he any man: But every man is tempted, when he is drawn away of his own lust, and enticed."

<u>I Timothy 6:9 </u>"But they that will be rich fall into temptation and a snare, and into many foolish and hurtful lusts, which drown men in destruction and perdition."

<u>I Corinthians 10:13</u> "There hath no temptation taken you but such as is common to man: but God is faithful, who will not suffer you to be tempted above that ye

are able; but will with temptation also make a way to escape, that ye may be able to bear it."

Trust

Psalm 37:3-5 "Trust in the Lord, and do good; so shalt thou dwell in the land, and verily thou shalt be fed. Delight thyself also in the Lord; and he shall give thee the desires of thine heart. Commit thy ways unto the Lord; trust also in him; and he shall bring it to pass."

2 Corinthians 1:9-10 "But we had the sentence of death in ourselves, but in God which raiseth the dead: Who delivered us from so great a death, and doth deliver: in whom we trust that he will yet deliver us;"

Proverbs 3:5-6 "Trust in the Lord with all thine heart; and lean not unto thine own understanding. In all thy ways acknowledge him, and he shall direct thy paths."

Jeremiah 17:7-8 "Blessed is the man that trusteth in the Lord, and whose hope the Lord is. For he shall be as a tree planted by the waters, and that spreadeth out her roots by the river, and shall not see when heat cometh, but her leaf shall be green; and shall not be careful in the year of drought, neither shall cease from yielding fruit."

<u>Psalm 84:11-12</u> "For the Lord God is a sun and shield: the Lord will give grace and glory: no good thing will he withhold from them that walk uprightly. O Lord of hosts, blessed is the man that trusteth in thee."

<u>Psalm 40:4</u> "Blessed is that man that maketh the Lord his trust, and respecteth not the proud, nor such as turn aside to lies."

<u>Psalm 34:8</u> "O taste and see that the Lord is good: blessed is the man that trusteth in him."

<u>Psalm 4:5</u> "Offer the sacrifices of righteousness, and put your trust in the Lord."

Weariness

<u>Galatians 6:9</u> "And let us not be weary in well doing: for in due season we shall reap, if we faint not."

<u>I Timothy 6:12</u> "Fight the good fight of faith, lay hold on eternal life, whereunto thou art also called, and hast professed a good profession before many witnesses."

<u>Ephesians 6:13</u> "Wherefore take unto you the whole armour of God, that ye may be able to withstand in the evil day, and having done all, to stand."

<u>Isaiah 40:28-29</u> "Hast thou not known? hast thou not heard, that the everlasting God, the Lord, the Creator of the ends of the earth, fainteth not, neither is weary? there is no searching of his understanding. He giveth power to the faint; and to them that have no might he increaseth strength."

<u>Proverbs 3:11</u> "My son, despise not the chastening of the Lord; neither be weary of his correction:"

<u>Job 3:17</u> "There the wicked cease from troubling; and there the weary be at rest."

<u>Isaiah 40:30-31</u> "Even the youths shall faint and be weary, and the young men shall utterly fall: But they that wait upon the Lord shall renew their strength; they shall mount up with wings as eagles; they shall run, and not be weary; and they shall walk, and not faint."

<u>Wisdom</u>
<u>James 1:5</u> "If any of you lack wisdom, let him ask of God, that giveth to all men liberally, and upbraideth not; and it shall be given him."

<u>Ecclesiastes 2:26</u> "For God giveth to a man that is good in his sight wisdom, and knowledge, and joy:"

<u>Matthew 11:19</u> "...But wisdom is justified of her children."

<u>Proverbs 4:5-6</u> "Get wisdom, get understanding: forget it not; neither decline from the words of my mouth. Forsake her not, and she shall preserve thee: love her, and she shall keep thee."

<u>Proverbs 16:16</u> "How much better is it to get wisdom than gold! And to get understanding rather to be chosen than silver!"

<u>Psalm 51:6</u> "Behold, thou desireth truth in the inward parts: and in the hidden part thou shalt make me to know wisdom."

<u>Proverbs 19:8</u> "He that getteth wisdom loveth his own soul: he that keepeth understanding shall find good."

<u>Proverbs 2:6-7</u> "For the Lord giveth wisdom: out of his mouth cometh knowledge and understanding. He layeth up sound wisdom for righteous: he is a buckler to them that walk uprightly."

<u>Deuteronomy 4:6-7</u> "Keep therefore and do them: for this is your wisdom and understanding in the sight of the nations, which shall hear all these statutes, and say, Surely this great nation is a wise and understanding

people. For what nation is there so great, who hath God so nigh unto them, as the Lord our God is in all things that we call upon him for?"

Word of God

Hebrews 4:12 "For the word of God is quick, and powerful, and sharper than any two edged sword, piercing even to the dividing asunder of soul and spirit, and the joints and marrow, and is a discerner of thoughts and intents of the heart."

I Peter 1:23 "Being born again, not of corruptible seed, but of incorruptible, by the word of God, which liveth and abideth forever."

Romans 10:17 "So then faith cometh by hearing, and hearing by the word of God."

Joshua 1:8 "This book of the law shall not depart out of thy mouth; but thou shalt meditate therein day and night, that thou mayest observe to do according to all that is written therein: for then thou shalt make thy way prosperous, and then thou shalt have good success."

Psalm 119:105 "Thy word is a lamp unto my feet, and a light unto my path."

Ephesians 5:25-26 "Husbands, love your wives, even as Christ also loved the Church, and gave himself for it; That he might sanctify and cleanse it with the washing of water by the Word,"

Colossians 3:16 "Let the word of Christ dwell in you richly in all wisdom; teaching and admonishing one another in psalms and hymns and spiritual songs, singing with grace in your hearts to the Lord."

John 15:3 "Now ye are clean through the word which I have spoken unto you."

Work

Deuteronomy 28:12 "The Lord shall open unto thee his good treasure, the heaven to give the rain unto thy land in his season, and to bless all the work of thine hand: and thou shalt lend unto many nations, and thou shalt not borrow."

I Corinthians 15:58 "Therefore, my beloved brethren, be ye steadfast, unmoveable, always abounding in the work of the Lord, forasmuch as ye know that your labour is not in vain in the Lord."

Ephesians 4:28 "Let him that stole steal no more: but rather let him labour, working with his hands the thing which is good, that he may have to give to him that needeth."

Proverbs 20:11 "Even a child is known by his doings, whether his work be pure, and whether it be right."

Proverbs 14:23 "In all labour there is profit: but the talk of the lips tendeth only to penury."

2 Chronicles 31:21 "And in every work that he began in the service of the house of God, and in the law, and in the commandments, to seek his God, he did it with all his heart, and prospered."

Proverbs 21:5 "The thoughts of the diligent tend only to plenteousness; but of every one that is hasty only to want."

Proverbs 21:25 "The desire of the slothful killeth him; for his hands refuse to labour."

Proverbs 22:29 "Seest thou a man diligent in his business? he shall stand before kings; he shall not stand before mean men."

Proverbs 23:4 "Labour not be rich: cease from thine own wisdom."

Proverbs 28:19 "He that tilleth his land shall have plenty of bread: but he that followeth after vain persons shall have poverty enough."

Worry

Philippians 4:6-7 "Be careful for nothing; but in everything by prayer and supplication with thanksgiving let your request be made known unto God. And the peace of God, which passeth all understanding, shall keep your hearts and minds through Christ Jesus."

2 Corinthians 4:8-9 "We are troubled on every side, yet not distressed; we are perplexed, but not in despair; Persecuted, but not forsaken; cast down, but not destroyed:"

Psalm 91:15 "He shall call upon me, and I will answer him: I will be with him in trouble; I will deliver him, and honour him."

Luke 10:41-42 "And Jesus answered and said unto her, Martha, Martha, thou art careful and troubled about many things: But one thing is needful; and Mary hath chosen that good part, which shall not be taken away from her."

<u>Psalm 91:9-10</u> "Because thou hast made the Lord, which is my refuge, even the Most High, thy habitation; There shall no evil befall thee, neither shall any plague come nigh thy dwelling."

<u>Psalm 91:1-2</u> "He that dwelleth in the secret place of the Most High shall abide under the shadow of the Almighty. I will say of the Lord, He is my refuge and my fortress: my God; in him will I trust."

<u>Psalm 46:1</u> "God is our refuge and strength, a very present help in trouble."

<u>Worship</u>
<u>John 4:23-24</u> "But the hour cometh, and now is, when the true worshippers shall worship the Father in spirit and in truth; for the Father seeketh such to worship him. God is a Spirit: and they that worship him must worship him in spirit and in truth."

<u>Psalm 86:9</u> "All nations whom thou hast made shall come and worship before thee, O Lord; and shall glorify thy name."

<u>Psalm 99:9</u> "Exalt the Lord our God, and worship at his holy hill; for the Lord our God is holy."

<u>Psalm 100:4</u> "Enter into his gates with thanksgiving, and into his courts with praise: be thankful unto him, and bless his name."

<u>Psalm 66:4</u> "All the earth shall worship thee, and shall sing unto thee; they shall sing to thy name."

<u>Revelation 11:16-17</u> "And the four and twenty elders, which sat before God on their seats, fell upon their faces, and worshipped God, Saying, we give thanks, O Lord God Almighty, which art, and wast, and art to come; because thou hast taken to thee thy great power, and hast reigned."

<u>Revelation 15:4</u> "Who shall not fear thee, O Lord, and glorify thy name? For thou art holy: for all nations shall come and worship before thee; for thy judgments are made manifest."

<u>Psalm 95:6-7</u> "O come, let us worship and bow down: let us kneel before the Lord our maker. For he is our God; and we are the people of his pasture, and the sheep of his hand..."

<u>Psalm 7:17</u> "I will praise the Lord according to his righteousness: and will sing praise to the name of the Lord most high."

Shawn Patrick Williams

CHAPTER SIX

EVERYDAY VICTORY FOR EVERYDAY PEOPLE

What is the secret to living in constant victory with God? How can anybody live in constant victory? Perhaps someone can live in increasing victory, but constant victory? Come on Brother Shawn Patrick, do you really believe that a person can live in constant victory with God?

Many people that have read the subtitle of *Warring with the Word* have asked those same questions. My answer to you is "Yes!" Yes, you can live in constant victory with God in the everyday situations of your life. God gives everyday victory to everyday people. And you are no different.

2 Corinthians 2:14 says, "Now thanks be unto God, which always causeth us to triumph in Christ and maketh manifest the savour of his knowledge by us in every place." The Vine's Complete Expository Dictionary[1] defines triumph as "to lead in triumph. Those who are led are not captives exposed to humiliation, but are displayed as the glory and devoted

subjects of Him who leads." What is the knowledge God is making manifest by us (the Believer) in every place? That knowledge is the fact that through Christ (the knowledge of His written Word and the empowerment of His Holy Spirit) we always have triumphant victory in every place and situation. That is everyday victory for everyday people!

During the first few years of my Christian life, I exercised my faith on protection and deliverance. Breaking ties with the occult was the area in which I needed breakthrough the most. Once I saw the power and victory that faith in God's Word brought in that area, I understood the victory that I could have as a Believer in Christ.

After experiencing the wonderful victory of Christ in other areas, I found other powerful scriptures of prosperity and peace. I began to apply the scriptures of sowing and reaping, joy, and intimacy with the Holy Spirit in faith. God began to change my personal relationships into the most exciting and pure relationships I had ever had.

I had always longed for a very personal relationship with my parents. I began to pray and confess the Word of God in my relationship with my parents. Then, in a few short months, God changed my situation. My relationship with my parents became that of best friends.

Shortly after this restoration of relationships with my family, I started being mentored by an evangelist, Reverend William "Billy" Mayo. He had been preaching a message called, "The Journey Thru Rock" all over the nation for 20 years. Back in the 80s, he was one of the first preachers to expose satanic lyrics in Rock-n-roll through "backward masking."

Backward masking is a process in which a song is played backward and hidden subliminal satanic messages are heard in the music and media. Billy's experience with the occult was much greater than most ministers in the United States. Because of this it made the discipleship process much easier for me, considering the nature of my situation.

During the first two years of training under Billy's ministry, I began to apply the scriptures on prosperity, sowing and reaping, and budgeting to my personal finances. In just a short time period my family went from barely getting by to experiencing a substantial increase in all of our assets. It was amazing to see God's promises come to pass for me in my everyday life. Everyday people can have everyday victory!

One night after preaching, a man came to me. He said, "You don't know what I've been through. How can you tell me I can have victory in all things? I've tried everything in the book and I just can't win the battle." I listened intently to the man for a few minutes while he offered all the reasons why he was defeated in his situation. I simply stated back, "But, Sir, you must understand you've already won the battle in Christ Jesus." You must come to the place in which you believe what the Word of God says about your situation, rather than what your physical circumstances look like. My friend, when you have this realization your life will never be the same.

One person who came to this realization was the Apostle Paul. He said in Romans 8:37, "Nay, in all these things we are more than conquerors through him that loved us." Here is a man who had been shipwrecked, beaten, stoned, and imprisoned. He said in the two verses before that it doesn't matter what "tribulation, or distress, or persecution, or famine, or nakedness, or peril, or sword" comes on your life, you are more than a conqueror. How can a man who has experienced all these hardships of life tell me I am more than a conqueror in all situations and have everyday victory in everyday life?

This is the revelation Paul had. No matter what happened to him, he always came out the victor. There is no victory where there is no battle. You can't be more than a conqueror without conquering something. Jesus told us in John 16:33, "In the world ye shall have tribulation: but be of good cheer; I have overcome the world."

The fact is every born again, blood-washed, Spirit-filled child of God will experience battles. The secret to living in constant victory during battles is knowing that when the dust settles, the Word of God will always prevail.

No matter how bad today might seem, your hope in God's Word will bring the manifestation of victory that you need into your life! Everyday people can have everyday victory!

Notes:
[1]*Vine'sComplete Expository Dictionary of Old And New Testament Words. (1ˢᵗ Ed.). (1996). Nashville, TN: Thomas Nelson, Inc.*

Shawn Patrick Williams

WHAT DOES IT MEAN TO BE "SAVED"?

"That if thou shalt confess with thy mouth the Lord Jesus, and shalt believe in thine heart that God raised him from the dead, thou shalt be saved" Romans 10:9.

The word "saved" in this verse is literally translated in Greek, sōzō, and it means to be made completely whole. If you verbally acknowledge Jesus Christ as your Lord and Savior, and believe that He was raised from the dead for the forgiveness of your sins, and to give you eternal life, you can be made whole physically, mentally, and spiritually. Only believe.

A Prayer of Salvation

Dear God, I believe Jesus died on the cross for my sins and was raised from the dead on the third day. I ask You to forgive me of all my sins past and present. I turn from my sins and ask Jesus Christ to come into my body, soul, and spirit. I confess Jesus Christ as my Lord and Savior and ask You to cleanse me with Your blood. I ask You, O God, to completely fill me with your Holy Spirit that I may know what it means to be "born again." I thank You for deliverance in every area of my life and I ask You these things in the name of Jesus Christ. Amen.

"I have written unto you, young men, because ye are strong, and the word of God abideth in you, and ye have overcome the wicked one."

I John 2:14

IT'S TIME TO
LIVE IN VICTORY!

- *Are you beaten down and tired because of the spiritual warfare in your life?*
- *Does it seem like you are in a constant endless cycle of defeat in your life?*
- *Is the stress of everyday life, circumstances, and daily spiritual warfare pulling on your family, depleting your finances, and deflating your faith?*
- *If you answered yes to any of these questions, this book is for you!*

Warring with the Word gives you secrets to living in constant victory with God. It gives you powerful revelation teachings on lasting victorious spiritual warfare that will enable you to see victory in every area of your life. Shawn Patrick Williams, ex-drug dealer to the occult, brings his personal experiences of lasting victorious spiritual warfare coming out of the occult, as well as many other real life spiritual warfare experiences, to enable you to unlock the secret to living in constant victory with God in everyday life.

Warrior Nations International Ministries, Inc. in Greenwood, SC. WNIM is the home of Shawn Patrick's evangelistic outreaches. Shawn Patrick is also the Pastor of Faith Family Harvest Church and is heavily involved in youth outreach programs, as well as mentoring programs.

To contact Shawn Patrick Williams write:

WARRIOR NATIONS PUBLICATIONS
PO Box 2352
Greenwood, South Carolina

To order additional copies of this book or to see a complete list of all **ADVANTAGE BOOKS™** visit our online bookstore at:

www.advbookstore.com

or For Book Orders Only, call our toll free order number at:

1-888-383-3110

Longwood, Florida, USA

"we bring dreams to life"™
www.advbooks.com

Printed in the United States
211529BV00001B/2/A